COME ON OVER!

COME ON OVER!

SOUTHERN DELICIOUS FOR EVERY DAY

 *&*

EVERY OCCASION

HOUGHTON MIFFLIN HARCOURT | BOSTON NEW YORK 2021

For information about permission to reproduce selections from this book, write
to trade.permissions@hmhco.com or to Permissions, Houghton Mifflin Harcourt
Publishing Company,
3 Park Avenue, 19th Floor, New York, New York 10016.
hmhbooks.com

Library of Congress Cataloging-in-Publication Data
Names: Heiskell, Elizabeth, author. | Mosier, Angie, photographer.
Title: Come on over! : Southern delicious for every day : every occasion /
Elizabeth Heiskell ; photography by Angie Mosier.
Description: Boston : Houghton Mifflin Harcourt, 2020. | Includes index.
Identifiers: LCCN 2020023891 (print) | LCCN 2020023892 (ebook) | ISBN
9780358248095 (hbk) | ISBN 9780358243915 (ebk)
Subjects: LCSH: Cooking, American—Southern style. | LCGFT: Cookbooks.
Classification: LCC TX715.2.S68 H44 2020 (print) | LCC TX715.2.S68   (ebook) |
DDC 641.5975—dc23
LC record available at https://lccn.loc.gov/2020023891
LC ebook record available at https://lccn.loc.gov/2020023892

Book design by Alissa Faden

Printed in China
SCP 10 9 8 7 6 5 4 3 2 1

For Momma and Daddy,
your love and encouragement from day one
has made all the difference in my life.

CONTENTS

☞

IT'S OFTEN
SUGGESTED THAT YOU
CAN TAKE THE GIRL
OUT OF THE DELTA,
BUT YOU CAN'T TAKE
THE DELTA OUT
OF THE GIRL.

Introduction

LET ME SAY, I've tested this hypothesis over the last few years with the nonstop travel and frenetic schedule required to film monthly segments as a contributor on the *TODAY* show and to promote two best-selling cookbooks—*What Can I Bring?* and *The Southern Living Party Cookbook*. In between countless book signings, radio interviews, and television appearances, I've racked up thousands of airline miles jetting back and forth between Mississippi and New York. Needless to say, I may be MIA in Mississippi more and more these days, but the Delta is with me wherever I go and is an element I bring to every appearance. The Delta accents my speech, flavors my recipes, serves as the setting for my stories, and informs much of what I do because it's in my DNA. The more I travel, the more I appreciate where I come from, and I am always happy to return home.

Come On Over! is all about home and the way I cook when I'm not catering an event for 2,500, demonstrating five camera-ready dishes on live television, or trying to keep up with orders for my popular Debutante Farmer Bloody Mary Mix. It's really about how I celebrate the everyday.

Growing up in the Delta, you had to make your own fun. We really only had three restaurants in town when I was coming along. We called them the three O's: Lello's, Doe's, and Lusco's. So we just cooked up our own fun. The way I see it, if you are

waiting for Christmas or New Year's Eve to celebrate, you will be one bored and lonely soul the rest of the time. Hell, there are 365 days in a year—that's 365 opportunities to let loose and enjoy. So what if it's just a Monday night? Go outside and clip a few flowers from your yard (or your neighbor's if they happen to be away on vacation) and bring them inside to arrange in a pretty vase on your dinner table. Use the nice cloth napkins. What are you saving them for anyway? Or why not make Wednesday nights a little more special? Let your kids invite their friends over for the "good chicken" (page 20). You'll definitely get brownie points for being a cool mom. My point is: It doesn't take much effort to make a meal or any average day a little more special. I will never forget dropping by to visit my great-grandmother one day as she was just about to sit down for lunch. Her table was set with cut crystal, fine china, and an abundance of fresh flowers. I asked if someone was coming over to have lunch with her.

She quickly responded, "No one is coming to my table who is more important than me."

Those words shaped me and shape how I choose to live in this world.

So, people, take the plastic off of the furniture in the living room and cook a beef tenderloin with a fancy sauce. Who cares if it's just a regular old Thursday? There are a helluva lot more Thursdays in a year than Thanksgivings. Live a lot and celebrate it all. If my first book, *What Can I Bring?*, is all about portable nibbles, crowd-pleasing casseroles, and from-scratch gifts for the host, and my second, *The Southern Living Party Cookbook*, shares inspired menus for entertaining, then it seems a natural progression that this is the book that serves up everything else. In these pages you will find the recipes my oldest daughter begs me to make when

she's on break from college, the dishes my husband, Luke, requests when our girls have scattered and our nest is empty, and the ones my momma made for me that bring me comfort and joy when I need a boost. Now, don't get me wrong, I will remain a party girl until my dying day, but in this book, I challenge cooks to celebrate every day: ho-hum weekdays, game days, diet days, cheat days, summer days, party days . . . any ole dadgum day! After all, life is short. I truly believe that every day should be savored.

1

WEEKDAYS

Ugh, Monday. Tolerating Tuesday. Wednesday—hump day. Thursday—almost Friday. Friday, just one more day . . . Saturday, celebrate! Sunday morning—delightful. Sunday night the Monday dread begins. Lord, just thinking about the way so many people view their weekdays makes my stomach hurt. I have a very busy catering company so my weeks look a little different: Our biggest days are Friday and Saturday, so Monday is one of my favorite days. It was on one of these Mondays that I attended a practice run for a James Beard dinner—a prestigious guest-chef event in New York City—at one of my favorite restaurants in Oxford, Saint Leo, before the chefs decamped for the actual event. I sat across from one of my most adorable friends, Jessica, who has more style in her pinkie than most have in their whole bodies and was holding a glass of rosé. I looked at her and said, "Not too bad for a Monday." I will never forget what she said: "Monday is just a word—only you can decide how you treat it." Truer words have never been spoken. Monday can be just as awesome as a Sunday morning. Thursday can be the most memorable day of the week. It's all up to you. Quit judging and labeling each day and just celebrate every one of them!

The Good Chicken

———◦◦◦◦◦———

At breakfast, it starts while the girls are midbite. They ask the dreaded question: "What's for supper?" The answer to this question will ultimately determine the true track of their day, good or bad. The first answer is chicken. But this is dicey because it can still go downhill from here. The middle child asks, "Is it the good chicken?" "Yes, the good chicken!" I reply, and the celebration begins. Even on a Wednesday, the right recipe can make all the difference. I am sure you are wondering what the "bad" chicken would be. Though it's super easy to prepare, the chicken that would sour my girls' moods faster than you can say "jumping jack rabbit" is a plain ole baked boneless, skinless chicken breast. Boring! This is the gussied-up chicken breast—served over steamed rice, mashed potatoes, or mashed cauliflower—that gets them excited for dinner.

SERVES 6

6 boneless, skinless chicken breasts

1 (1-ounce) packet ranch dressing mix

1 (1-ounce) packet gravy mix

1 (16-ounce) jar banana pepper rings, drained

¼ cup banana pepper juice from the jar

4 cups chicken broth, or more to cover the chicken

1. Place the chicken breasts in a slow cooker and sprinkle the dressing mix, gravy mix, peppers, and pepper juice over the chicken. Pour in chicken broth to cover the chicken.

2. Cover and cook on high for 4 hours or on low for 8 hours, until the chicken is tender and shreds easily with a fork.

3. To serve, slice or shred the chicken and spoon the sauce on top.

Mom Tip If you don't have a slow cooker, combine the ingredients in a Dutch oven or other deep, heavy pot with a tight-fitting lid. Bake in a 350°F oven for about 3 hours, until the chicken is tender.

Beef Bourguignon

I know, I know: it is a good thing Julia Child isn't alive to see this because the words "slow cooker" in front of her beloved beef bourguignon recipe would have surely killed her. But Julia Child didn't have three wild girls going in twenty different directions, three businesses, two dogs, and two cats. Even when life is hectic, you still want to make each crazy day special. Just say the words "beef bourguignon"—don't you already feel fancier? Set your morning alarm thirty minutes earlier to get this in the slow cooker before you start your day. I promise you will enjoy your dinner much more than the thirty minutes of sleep. Serve with Smashed Potatoes (page 25), if you like.

SERVES 6, WITH LEFTOVERS

5 slices bacon

3 pounds boneless beef chuck, cut into 1-inch cubes

Salt and pepper

1 cup red wine (save the rest of the bottle for sipping)

2 cups beef broth

½ cup tomato sauce

1½ teaspoons soy sauce

¼ cup all-purpose flour

3 cloves garlic, minced

2 teaspoons finely chopped fresh thyme

5 medium carrots, peeled and chopped into 2-inch pieces

8 ounces fresh white button mushrooms, wiped clean, stems removed

½ (14.5-ounce) bag frozen pearl onions

1 pound baby potatoes, scrubbed (optional; if serving over mashed potatoes, don't add these)

Fresh parsley, for garnish (optional)

1. In a large skillet, cook the bacon over medium-high heat until crisp. Cut the bacon into ½-inch pieces. Transfer the bacon to the slow cooker, leaving the grease in the skillet.

2. Generously season the beef with salt and pepper on all sides. (We eat all sides of the beef, we season all sides of the beef.) Working in batches if necessary, add the beef to the bacon grease and sear on all sides over medium-high heat for 2 to 3 minutes per side. Transfer the beef to the slow cooker.

Chef Tip As soon as the beef touches the skillet, it will stick. Relax. Don't get out your spatula and start scraping it off for fear of burning. Once it has a nice caramelized crust, the protein fibers will contract, and it will pull itself away from the pan. No panic or scraping necessary. Same goes for any protein, whether in a skillet or on an outdoor grill.

3. Add the red wine to the skillet to deglaze the pan. (That's a fancy way to say pour liquid in the pan and scrape the bottom with your wooden spoon to get all those flavor nuggets into your sauce.) Bring the wine to a simmer, then add the broth, tomato sauce, and soy sauce. Slowly whisk in the flour. Pour the sauce into the slow cooker.

4. Add the garlic, thyme, carrots, mushrooms, onions, and baby potatoes (if desired). Stir well. Cover and cook on high for 6 to 8 hours, until the beef is tender.

5. Garnish with parsley, unless your family or friends have an aversion to the "yucky green stuff."

SMASHED POTATOES

This is the quickest way to get the creamiest mashed potatoes ever.

SERVES 4 TO 6

10 large red-skinned new potatoes (about 2 pounds), scrubbed really well

4 tablespoons (½ stick) salted butter

6 ounces cream cheese, room temperature

½ cup milk or half-and-half

Salt and pepper

1. Place the potatoes in a large pot of water, making sure they are fully covered to ensure even cooking. Bring to a boil and cook until a knife can be inserted easily into a potato, 35 to 45 minutes, depending on how large the potatoes are.

2. Drain the potatoes and return them to the pot. Add the butter and cream cheese. Allow the butter and cheese to melt a little bit. Add the milk and season with salt and pepper.

3. Using a potato masher, mash until all ingredients are well incorporated. Taste and adjust the seasoning as needed.

PERFECT
Roasted Chicken

Chicken and rice was one of the first dishes I ever cooked. You know the one: chicken, rice, a can of condensed "cream of X" soup (mushroom, celery, chicken, etc.). This roast chicken recipe honestly takes less time than that casserole, and, served with the Vidalia Onion and Artichoke Casserole on page 47, it's the perfect way to elevate any weeknight meal. This recipe is super simple, which means the techniques are very important. For crisp skin, make sure your chicken is absolutely dry. I even have friends that will use a ShamWow to dry it. Yes, the late-night infomercial towel for drying your car!! A blow-dryer is a great tool for this as well. I know it sounds funny! But seriously: Dry skin equals crisp skin.

SERVES 4 TO 6

8 tablespoons (1 stick) salted butter, room temperature

4 cloves garlic, minced

2 teaspoons finely chopped fresh thyme

1 tablespoon chopped fresh rosemary

1 lemon, zested and halved

1 teaspoon salt

1 teaspoon pepper

1 whole chicken

1 large onion, sliced into 1½-inch-thick rings

1. Preheat the oven to 450°F. Mix the butter, garlic, thyme, rosemary, lemon zest, ½ teaspoon of the salt, and ½ teaspoon of the pepper together in a bowl.

2. Rinse the chicken and pat dry. Loosen the skin on the breast. Rub herb butter between the skin and the breast meat, then over the outside of the bird. Sprinkle on the remaining salt and pepper. Squeeze the lemon over the chicken, then place the lemon halves inside the cavity.

3. Place the onion rings side by side in the middle of a rimmed baking sheet or roasting pan. Place the bird, breast-side up, on top of the onion. (This will elevate the chicken so that the skin will stay crisp on all sides, rather than getting soggy sitting in the juices.)

4. Roast for 15 minutes, then turn the heat down to 400°F. Roast until the chicken is no longer pink and the juices run clear when you insert a knife into the thigh joint, at least 1 hour more. (An instant-read thermometer should read 165°F.)

5. Transfer the chicken to a cutting board and let rest for 15 minutes. Using a very sharp knife, carve into pieces—legs, thighs, wings, back, and breast halves—and slice the breast meat. Don't let those delicious onions go to waste: Cut them up and top the chicken with them.

Cabbage

I wish I had some way to make sure that the sleeper recipes in this book don't get overlooked, maybe a scratch-and-sniff box or a pop-up page. This recipe would need both—it is just that good. There are only a few ingredients, but when done right it will become a weeknight sensation. It's all in the technique. Make sure your heat is medium; you want the cabbage to caramelize but not burn—there is a fine line. Be very careful and stir often.

SERVES 4

1 medium head green cabbage

2 tablespoons salted butter

2 tablespoons olive oil

1½ teaspoons kosher salt

½ teaspoon pepper

1. Cut the cabbage into quarters. (Any time you are cutting something like a ball that rolls, always give it a flat side to keep your fingers safe.) Cut the core out of the cabbage and discard it. Slice the cabbage crosswise as thin as possible.

2. Melt the butter and olive oil in a heavy-bottomed pot over medium heat. Add the cabbage, salt, and pepper and sauté until the cabbage begins to brown, 10 to 15 minutes. Adjust the seasoning to taste and serve immediately.

Soup and Sandwich Night

———◦◦◦◦◦———

There is absolutely nothing wrong with a grilled cheese sandwich and Campbell's tomato soup. But this book is all about making everyday food special. We can make this meal extraordinary with only a few more minutes and a little more effort. The great news is you probably have all the ingredients in your kitchen right now. If not, don't be afraid to make substitutions. No ham? No worries, use turkey. No turkey? No worries, use the veggies that are in your crisper. Be creative! It's not your last supper, so if it doesn't turn out to be the best ever, there's always tomorrow.

TOMATO SOUP

SERVES 4 TO 6

4 slices bacon, cut into small pieces

2 carrots, chopped

½ yellow onion, chopped

4 cloves garlic, minced

1½ tablespoons tomato paste with Italian herbs

1 tablespoon all-purpose flour

1 (28-ounce) can whole San Marzano tomatoes with basil

4 cups chicken broth

½ teaspoon dried basil or 1½ teaspoons chopped fresh basil

2 bay leaves

Salt and pepper

½ cup heavy cream (if you like—totally up to you)

1. Cook the bacon in a large soup pot or Dutch oven over medium-high heat, until it starts to crisp and brown, about 5 minutes. (Do not burn the bacon. If you do burn the bacon, start over.)

2. Add the carrots, onion, and garlic to the pan with the bacon. Sauté until the veggies are tender, 5 to 10 minutes. Add the tomato paste and stir until the paste just begins to brown. Add the flour and stir well.

3. Hold your hand over the pot and one at a time, pour the tomatoes into your hand. Gently squeeze the tomatoes to break them up, letting all the juice run through your fingers. Drop the crushed tomatoes into the pot. Add any juice left in the can, the broth, basil, bay leaves, and salt and pepper to taste. Let simmer for about 30 minutes.

4. Remove the bay leaves. Puree the soup in the pot using a hand blender, or in batches in a standard blender. (Be very careful, as the soup is hot and will burn your body if it spatters onto you.) If you used a standard blender, return the pureed soup to the pan. Add the cream if you'd like. Serve hot.

Mom Tip So many of my girlfriends are gluten-free, vegan, or vegetarian for health or ethical reasons. I admire them but I especially admire my daughter Lucia's best friend, Ellis, who is only sixteen years old and has been a vegan for three years. Ellis cooks for herself and does a meal prep that would make your head spin. She is strong and dedicated. To make the Ellis-style (vegan) version of this soup, and/or to make it gluten-free:

—No bacon; cook the vegetables in 2 tablespoons olive oil in step 2

—No flour and/or no cream

—Use vegetable broth

Is it still an amazing soup? Yes, ma'am, it is!

THE SANDWICH

2 sticks butter, plus more for grilling the sandwiches

1 onion, finely chopped

2 teaspoons Worcestershire sauce

3 tablespoons Dijon mustard

8 slices sturdy white bread

1 pound deli ham

1 pound swiss or provolone cheese, sliced

1. In a small saucepan, melt the butter. Add the onion, Worcestershire, and Dijon and cook until the onion is translucent, about 5 minutes.

2. Place the bread slices on the counter. On four slices, spread a layer of the onion mixture. Then divide the ham and cheese between the sandwiches. Top with the other four slices of bread.

3. Heat a medium skillet over medium heat. Spread one side of a sandwich with butter. Place butter-side down in the pan and cook until the bread is golden. Butter the second side of the sandwich, flip, and cook until golden and the cheese is melted. Repeat with the remaining sandwiches. Cut on the diagonal and serve with soup.

Chicken Tetrazzini

This is my all-time favorite dish that my mother used to make. Momma was a divine cook who never took a shortcut. Biscuits were from scratch. Pancakes, homemade. Hollandaise sauce, no blender required. She was old-school when it came to cooking. I will never forget the time I had Kraft boxed mac-n-cheese at a friend's house—I thought I had died and gone to heaven. I begged Momma to call and find out the mac-n-cheese recipe. When she hung up the phone, she said the mac-n-cheese was from a box and no, ma'am, not in this house. You will see that Momma's Chicken Tetrazzini recipe is devoid of green peas and pimento. If you love those, add them. For me it was always Momma's way or the highway, so I will stick to her recipe.

SERVES 6 TO 8

8 tablespoons (1 stick) salted butter

1 tablespoon olive oil

1 pound button mushrooms, wiped clean, stems removed, sliced

½ large onion, finely diced

5 cloves garlic, minced

1 teaspoon dried thyme

⅓ cup all-purpose flour

3 cups milk

2 cups heavy cream

1 cup chicken broth

⅛ teaspoon ground nutmeg

Salt and pepper

16 ounces thin spaghetti noodles

4 boneless, skinless chicken breasts, cooked and shredded (see Mom Tip, below)

½ cup grated parmesan cheese

¼ cup dried Italian-flavored bread crumbs (Momma made her own; don't dare tell her we took a shortcut)

Mom Tip So many easy casseroles and dishes start with shredded chicken breast. Well, when you come home from a long day, that's just one more step, which means you are one step closer to ordering pizza. So in the morning, take your chicken breasts, put them in your slow cooker, cover with chicken broth, and set on low for 8 hours. In the evening your chicken is perfectly cooked and ready to shred. Now, if you don't have a moment in the morning to breathe, much less find the slow cooker, simply buy a rotisserie chicken and pull the meat from it, and voilà, your meal is halfway done.

1. Preheat the oven to 350°F.

2. In a medium saucepan over medium heat, melt 1 tablespoon of the butter and the olive oil. Cook the mushrooms, onion, garlic, and thyme until the onion is tender, about 5 minutes. Remove the veggies from the pan and set aside.

3. Melt the remaining 7 tablespoons butter in the same pan. Add the flour and whisk for 2 minutes. Whisk in the milk, cream, broth, nutmeg, and a pinch each salt and pepper. Bring to a low boil and simmer until the sauce thickens, 8 to 10 minutes, continuing to whisk the entire time.

4. Meanwhile, bring a pot of salted water to a boil. Add the spaghetti and cook until tender but still firm (al dente), according to the package instructions. Drain the pasta well and then return it to the pot. Add the vegetables, sauce, and chicken and mix well. Pour into a 9 x 13-inch baking dish.

Chef Tip It is crucial to salt your water before boiling pasta. The water should be "as salty as seawater." This is so important because as soon as the dried pasta gets in the water it soaks up a ton of water. If the water is flavorless your pasta will be, too.

5. Stir together the cheese and bread crumbs and sprinkle over the top. Bake uncovered until golden brown and bubbly, about 30 minutes.

Farro and Salmon Bowls

If I tell my children that we are having salmon with farro for supper they will roll their eyes so far in the back of their head I worry their eyes just might stick, followed by a long sigh, hair flip, and defeated walk out of the kitchen. On the other hand, if I tell them we are having these farro and salmon bowls, big smiles will appear on their faces and they practically skip out of the room. It's all in the way you sell it. That's true for so many things in life, but especially when dealing with three teenage girls.

I will say this over and over: Cook double when making protein . . . that way you have a head start on your next meal. This is a prime example. Cook double the salmon on Monday, then Wednesday use the extra for this bowl or a quick, on-the-go lunch. I know this recipe looks like a lot, but if you use leftover salmon and make your dressing in big batches ahead of time, half the battle is done. It's so worth it, I promise.

SERVES 8

For the Salmon

3½ to 4 pounds skin-on salmon fillets (roughly 9 ounces per person)

3 tablespoons olive oil

Salt and pepper

1 lemon

Chef Tip Always buy wild-caught salmon. Even if it's frozen. There is no comparison in the nutritional value or the taste. Farm-raised salmon many times has antibiotics put in the water, it's virtually devoid of omega-3s, and, since the flesh is gray in color, dye is added to make it more marketable.

For the Dressing

¼ cup fresh lime juice

3 tablespoons fish sauce

1 tablespoon honey

1 tablespoon peeled and grated fresh ginger (a Microplane grater is perfect for this. Don't have one? Get one—it is invaluable in the kitchen.)

2 teaspoons red pepper flakes

3 tablespoons extra virgin olive oil or canola oil

For the Salad

4 cups shredded napa cabbage

3 cups thinly sliced bell peppers, any color (about 4 peppers)

3 cups thinly sliced peeled carrots

2 green onions, chopped (white and green parts)

¼ cup chopped fresh basil

¼ cup chopped fresh cilantro

For the Bowls

2 cups farro, cooked according to package instructions (about 4 cups cooked)

2 cups frozen shelled edamame, thawed

1 cup drained canned mandarin oranges

½ cup thinly sliced cucumber

¼ cup coarsely chopped roasted salted peanuts

Mom Tip If you are short on time, use slaw in the bag instead of chopping all the cabbage, carrots, and peppers—no judgment here. You didn't go through a drive-through or order takeout, you cooked for your family. If you need a little help to make that happen, so be it.

1. **COOK THE SALMON:** Heat the oven to 425°F. Line a rimmed baking sheet with foil or parchment paper.

2. Pat the salmon dry with a paper towel. Rub the salmon with the oil and place it skin-side down on the baking sheet. Sprinkle with salt and pepper. Cut the lemon and squeeze the juice over the salmon.

3. Roast for about 8 minutes, until the salmon flakes apart easily with a fork. Do not overcook. Set aside.

4. **MAKE THE DRESSING:** In a small bowl, whisk together the lime juice, fish sauce, honey, ginger, and red pepper flakes. Slowly drizzle the oil and keep whisking until it is thick and well blended (or in chef-speak, emulsified).

5. **MAKE THE SALAD:** In a large bowl, mix the cabbage, peppers, carrots, green onions, basil, cilantro, and enough of the dressing to coat but not drown the cabbage.

6. **ASSEMBLE THE BOWLS:** Divide the cooked farro between soup bowls. Place the cabbage mixture to one side of each bowl. Divide the salmon, edamame, oranges, and cucumber between the four bowls. Top with peanuts and serve.

Alfredo

WITH PEPPERS, ONIONS, AND SAUSAGE

My mother is extremely health-oriented. She always has been. When we were growing up, we only had skim milk. The best cereal we ever got was Raisin Bran. I will never forget how excited we were when Momma brought home a cereal we'd never had before, called Grape-Nuts. We just knew it would be fantastic (umm, not so much). No ice cream for our household; we got ice milk— that would be ice cream made with skim milk. So how, then, do you explain that we had Fettuccine Alfredo with Italian sausage and peppers at least twice a week? To this day, I cannot figure it out. As if the Fettuccine Alfredo wasn't fattening and heart-stopping enough, let's add some Italian sausage to it. I guess we all have our weaknesses and Momma's vices were pasta, cream, and sausage.

SERVES 6

6 (4-ounce) links Italian sausage

½ pound (2 sticks) plus 2 tablespoons salted butter

1½ yellow onions, thinly sliced

4 cloves garlic, minced

2 large green bell peppers, thinly sliced (you can use one red one if you like, but in the '70s in Rosedale, Mississippi, we were lucky to find any peppers at all, much less a red one)

1 teaspoon dried oregano

1 teaspoon dried basil

¼ cup dry white wine

24 ounces fettuccine noodles

¾ cup heavy cream

Salt and pepper

2¼ cups grated parmesan cheese

1. Place the sausages in a skillet and brown on all sides over medium heat, turning once, about 15 minutes total. Remove from the skillet, slice into 1-inch pieces, and set aside.

2. Melt 2 tablespoons of the butter in the skillet. Stir in the onions and garlic. Cook for 2 to 3 minutes, until slightly softened. Add the bell peppers, oregano, basil, and wine. Cook, stirring occasionally, until the onions and peppers are tender. Return the sausage to the skillet and cook over low heat until the sausage is cooked through, about 10 minutes. Set aside.

3. Meanwhile, bring a large pot of salted water to a boil. Cook the fettuccine until tender, about 10 minutes. Drain.

4. In a large saucepan, combine the remaining ½ pound butter and the cream over low heat. Season with salt and pepper. Stir in the cheese until melted and the sauce has thickened slightly. Add the fettuccine to the sauce. Divide the pasta among plates and top with the sausages and peppers.

Chicken Divan
(OR DIVINE)

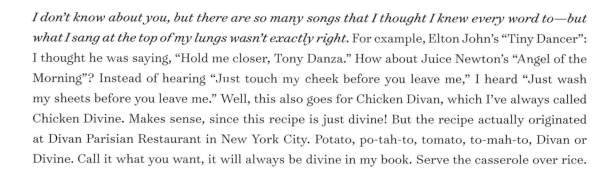

I don't know about you, but there are so many songs that I thought I knew every word to—but what I sang at the top of my lungs wasn't exactly right. For example, Elton John's "Tiny Dancer": I thought he was saying, "Hold me closer, Tony Danza." How about Juice Newton's "Angel of the Morning"? Instead of hearing "Just touch my cheek before you leave me," I heard "Just wash my sheets before you leave me." Well, this also goes for Chicken Divan, which I've always called Chicken Divine. Makes sense, since this recipe is just divine! But the recipe actually originated at Divan Parisian Restaurant in New York City. Potato, po-tah-to, tomato, to-mah-to, Divan or Divine. Call it what you want, it will always be divine in my book. Serve the casserole over rice.

SERVES 6 TO 8

1½ pounds fresh broccoli, cut into spears

1½ cups shredded cheddar cheese

¾ cup milk

⅔ cup sour cream

1 (10.5 ounce) can condensed "cream of X" soup (any kind—mushroom, celery—will do)

½ teaspoon garlic powder

½ teaspoon onion powder

½ teaspoon dry mustard

½ teaspoon curry powder (this is completely optional—Momma used it, I think, because it made her feel very exotic.)

¼ teaspoon seasoned salt

Pepper

3 cups shredded cooked chicken (see Mom Tip, page 33)

1 cup bread crumbs

2 tablespoons salted butter, melted

1. Preheat the oven to 400°F.

2. Bring a large pot of salted water to a boil and add the broccoli. Cook until crisp-tender, about 8 minutes. (Do not overcook; remember, you will be cooking it again in your casserole.)

3. In a medium bowl, combine 1 cup of the cheddar cheese, the milk, sour cream, soup, garlic powder, onion powder, dry mustard, curry powder (if using), seasoned salt, and pepper to taste. Stir in the broccoli and chicken. Spread in a 9 x 13-inch baking dish and top with the remaining cheese.

4. In a small bowl, mix the bread crumbs and butter. Sprinkle the topping over the chicken mixture. Bake until lightly browned and bubbly, about 20 minutes.

Chicken and Dumplings

One of the most soul-satisfying meals I ever had was chicken and dumplings, prepared by my great friend Deloris. It was after Christmas one year and I was absolutely exhausted, my stomach ulcer was killing me, and I could hardly get out of bed. Deloris made me her famous chicken and dumplings: She simmered a whole chicken with carrots, onions, and celery for hours—the meat literally fell off the bones, it was so tender. Then she carefully made her dumplings. She added the chicken back to the broth and, with as much care as you can imagine, placed the dumplings in the broth. Then she let the soup simmer and thicken. I can still remember the way it tasted—but what I can remember most is how it made me feel. I literally felt it in my soul.

Now, the recipe that follows isn't Deloris's recipe. But I promise you can get the same soul-soothing feeling with this slow-cooker version of chicken and dumplings. Sometimes it's not about the method; it's about the results.

SERVES 8

2 pounds boneless, skinless chicken breasts or thighs

1 yellow onion, diced

1 clove garlic, minced

2 (10.5-ounce) cans condensed cream of mushroom soup

3 cups chicken broth, plus more if you like

1 teaspoon poultry seasoning

1 teaspoon pepper

1 (8-count) tube refrigerated biscuit dough

Mom Tip I have to tell you, I avoid canned cream of chicken soup at all costs. In the ingredient list it says, "mechanically separated chicken parts." That is entirely too violent and vague for me. I use cream of mushroom across the board.

1. Combine the chicken, onion, garlic, soup, broth, poultry seasoning, and pepper in a slow cooker. Cover and cook on high for 3 hours or low for 6 hours.

2. When the chicken is cooked through and super tender, shred the meat and put it back in the slow cooker. Stir to combine.

3. To make the dumplings, open the tube of biscuits and press each biscuit down until it is 1 inch flat. Cut them into narrow strips, about 5 strips per biscuit. Add the biscuit strips to the slow cooker. Stir to combine.

4. Cover and cook on high for 1 hour, or until the dumplings are cooked through. When you think about it, stir to make sure all the dumplings are submerged in the broth. If you like your chicken and dumplings more souplike, you can always add a little more broth.

My Spaghetti

I believe everybody has one dish that they are really proud of. That one thing that when you make it you know everyone is going to have to have it. So seriously good that if you had a flashing sign outside above your door it would read "Home of the World's Best X." Well, this is my "world's best" dish: my spaghetti sauce. It is loosely based on my mother's and grandmother's Bolognese sauce. Cue the marquee, "Home of the World-Famous Spaghetti Sauce," and get to cooking.

This recipe is already doubled for you. I always freeze half the sauce. It's the perfect base for lasagna or the Spaghetti Pie on page 49. Having spaghetti sauce in the freezer is like having good insurance—always there when you need it. And trust me, you will need it!

SERVES 8, WITH EXTRA TO STORE

5 pounds ground chuck

3 tablespoons olive oil

1 large yellow onion, chopped (about 3 cups)

4 cloves garlic, chopped

1 stalk celery, finely chopped

½ carrot, peeled and chopped so fine it's unrecognizable

1 (14.5-ounce) can crushed tomatoes

1 (6-ounce) can tomato paste with Italian herbs

1 (8-ounce) can tomato sauce

3 bay leaves

1 teaspoon dried oregano

1 teaspoon dried basil

½ teaspoon dried parsley

4 cups beef broth, maybe a little more to thin the sauce as it cooks down

Salt and pepper

1 (1-pound) package very thin spaghetti noodles

4 tablespoons (½ stick) salted butter

1. Heat a Dutch oven or other large heavy-bottomed pot over medium heat. Cook the beef, stirring often, until crumbled and no longer pink, about 15 minutes. Remove the meat with a slotted spoon and set aside; pour the grease into the trash.

2. Add the oil to the same pot and then add the onion, garlic, celery, and carrot. Sauté until the onion is translucent, about 8 minutes.

3. Add back the cooked beef and stir in the tomatoes, tomato paste, tomato sauce, bay leaves, oregano, basil, parsley, and broth. Bring to a boil and boil for about 10 minutes, then turn the heat down to low. Simmer for at least 30 minutes, or 1 to 2 hours if you have that much time; the longer it cooks, the more intense the flavors will get. Since the broth can be very salty, taste the sauce before adding salt, then season to taste with pepper. Remove the bay leaves.

4. Boil the spaghetti in a large pot of salted water according to the package instructions until tender. Drain well. Pour the pasta back into the pot. Add 4 to 5 cups of the sauce (about half of the sauce) and then the butter. Mix well and serve.

Chef Tip When substituting fresh herbs for dried herbs, always remember that dried herbs are three times more potent than fresh. When the moisture is removed during the drying process, the herb's flavor is concentrated. The good news is that all dried herbs can withstand a long cooking process and keep their flavor. Fresh herbs, on the other hand, have a big burst of flavor and then that flavor dies. Neither is better than the other. Just remember to add fresh herbs at the very end of the cooking time in order to maximize their flavor burst.

VIDALIA ONION AND ARTICHOKE
Casserole

This recipe comes from my best friend, Amanda; it was her grandmother's. Her grandma Hazel Sanders was the epitome of everything lovely about the Delta—gracious, beautiful, and welcoming. She was so pretty that she didn't have to cook to make her sweet husband happy, but she did anyway. Some people are just overachievers. She made this casserole to celebrate Vidalia onion season—those months, starting in the early spring, when the super-sweet Georgia onions are available. I am not sure what it is about Southern grandmothers and their onions but when my husband, Luke, and I were dating, a huge box of Vidalia onions arrived from his grandma Betty. The next day an envelope arrived, also from Grandma Betty, containing panty hose and a note addressed to me. In the letter, she wanted to make sure I knew the panty hose were from her and not another one of Luke's girlfriends! Then she went on to say that she sent them for Luke to tie up the onions in. You see, this is the perfect way to store the prized Vidalia onions. It keeps them from touching one another, so they keep longer. Drop an onion in the leg of the panty hose, tie a knot, and continue—onion, knot, onion, knot—then hang the onion-filled panty hose in a cool, dry place. As you need an onion, cut off the knot below so the onion falls out. Grandma Betty was a genius.

SERVES 6 TO 8

2 cups long-grain white rice

8 tablespoons (1 stick) unsalted butter

4 cups finely chopped Vidalia onions (about 2 large onions)

3 (14-ounce) cans chicken broth

2 cups artichoke hearts (two 14-ounce cans, drained), chopped

1½ cups grated parmesan cheese

1. Preheat the oven to 350°F. Rinse the rice in a fine-mesh strainer under cold running water and drain. (This helps get rid of any extra starch.)

2. Melt the butter over medium heat in a large skillet. Add the onions and cook, stirring often, until the onions are softened, 10 to 12 minutes. Stir in the rice and cook until the rice is toasted, about 2 minutes.

3. Stir in the broth, artichoke hearts, and 1 cup of the parmesan. Transfer to a 9 x 13-inch baking dish. Sprinkle the remaining ½ cup cheese on top. Cover and bake until the liquid has been absorbed and the rice is tender, 45 minutes to 1 hour.

Spaghetti Pie

This is my adaptation of TV host Adam Richman's recipe. When Adam made his spaghetti pie on the *TODAY* show it went viral. It's one of their top requested recipes. After making my own version, I had to agree it was pretty fantastic. Serve it with a green salad and garlic bread.

SERVES 6

12 ounces dried spaghetti noodles, cooked al dente and drained

3 large eggs, lightly beaten

1 cup grated parmesan cheese

1½ cups shredded mozzarella cheese

¼ cup tomato paste

2 tablespoons olive oil

4 cups sauce from My Spaghetti (page 45; about ½ recipe)

1. Preheat the oven to 350°F.

2. In a large bowl, mix together the spaghetti, eggs, parmesan, 1 cup of the mozzarella, and the tomato paste.

3. Grease a 9- or 10-inch deep-dish pie pan with the olive oil. Spread half the spaghetti sauce in the bottom. Top with the noodle mixture and press to make the noodles even. Top with the remaining sauce. Sprinkle the remaining ½ cup mozzarella on top.

4. Bake for 30 to 35 minutes, until the top is golden and the pie is warmed through. Let sit at room temperature for 10 minutes, then slice like a pie with a sharp knife.

Pork Shoulder

There are those who stay away from cooking large cuts of meat. I get it—if the roast is bigger than your own head, it can be intimidating. But this recipe will show you what a walk in the park it can be. The best news is you will have leftover for days. The leftover pork can be transformed into street tacos, Brunswick stew, pork enchiladas, or BBQ sliders.

Pork can be dry and tough if not cooked properly. But if you cook it low and slow, it can be the juiciest meat in the barnyard. This recipe is perfect for an alfresco supper under the stars; serve it with grilled vegetables. Talk about a wonderful backyard weeknight.

SERVES 8, WITH LEFTOVERS

4 large dried ancho chiles (3 to 4 ounces total), stemmed and seeded

2 large dried chiles de arbol or japones chiles, stemmed and seeded

2 tablespoons sugar

1 tablespoon fresh lime juice

1 (5-pound) boneless pork shoulder (Boston butt)

Kosher salt

2 tablespoons vegetable oil

1 large onion, chopped (about 2 cups)

3 large cloves garlic, coarsely chopped

2 bay leaves

2 teaspoons dried oregano

2 teaspoons ground coriander

2 teaspoons ground cumin

½ teaspoon ground allspice

1 (12-ounce) bottle dark beer

1. Place the chiles in a medium bowl. Add enough boiling water to cover and set a small plate or bowl on the chiles to keep them submerged. Let the chiles soak until softened, about 30 minutes. Drain the chiles, reserving 1 cup of the soaking liquid.

2. Meanwhile, preheat the oven to 350°F.

3. Place the chiles, sugar, lime juice, and ¼ cup of the reserved soaking liquid in a blender. Puree the chile mixture, adding more soaking liquid as needed to form a smooth paste.

4. Season the pork shoulder generously with salt and spread the chile paste over the pork. (You can do this 1 to 2 days ahead; cover and refrigerate. Let the pork come to room temperature before continuing.)

5. Heat the oil in a large heavy pot or Dutch oven over medium heat. Add the onion, garlic, bay leaves, oregano, coriander, cumin, and allspice. Cook, stirring often, until the onion is soft, about 8 minutes. Add the beer and bring to a boil.

6. Add the pork, cover, and transfer to the oven. Braise the pork, basting occasionally with the pan juices, until very tender, about 2½ hours. To serve, shred the meat off the bone.

Mom Tip You could also cook this in a slow cooker instead of the oven. In step 5, cook in a large skillet. In step 6, put the pork in the slow cooker, pour over the contents of the skillet, cover, and cook on low for 8 hours or on high for 6 hours.

VANILLA BEAN ICE CREAM WITH
Bing Cherries and Wine Syrup

———◇∞◇———

When we were little, we never had dessert at home. Momma didn't eat desserts, so I guess she figured no one else needed them. She was a health nut before there was such a thing. Had she not been born in the Mississippi Delta, I am pretty sure she would have joined a commune and lived on granola, hemp, and alfalfa sprouts. The one exception was on our birthdays. But I honestly cannot think of a better way to liven up a boring weeknight than serving dessert. Let's end this meal with an exclamation point, not a period! This dessert couldn't be simpler. The ice cream man did half the work, all you have to do is make the sauce.

SERVES 4

1 pound frozen dark sweet cherries, thawed, pitted, and drained, juices reserved

¼ cup Kirsch or clear brandy

¼ cup dry red wine

3 tablespoons sugar

1 tablespoon cornstarch

⅛ teaspoon almond extract (optional)

1½ pints vanilla bean ice cream

1. Pour the juices from the cherries into a measuring cup. Add the Kirsch and red wine.

2. Stir together the sugar and cornstarch in a small saucepan until no lumps remain. Gradually whisk in the wine mixture. Add the cherries. Cook over medium heat until the sauce boils and thickens, about 5 minutes. Remove from heat and add the almond extract (if desired). Let cool slightly.

3. Serve the warm sauce over the ice cream.

CARAMEL HEATH BAR
Trifle

———◆◇◆———

This delicious dessert actually came about out of sheer horror and panic. I will never forget the day: My catering team and I were in the "prison van" (my catering van) headed to a client's home for a lovely dinner party, with chocolate pots de crème for dessert. The person in front of us slammed on their brakes, and to avoid an accident we slammed on ours. Well, that was all she wrote for the pots de crème. They were everywhere. I had to find another dessert, and fast. So we gathered our thoughts, exhaled, and high-tailed to the Kroger. I found a bakery chocolate Bundt cake, Heath Bar toffee bits, caramel sauce, chocolate sauce, vanilla ice cream, and heavy cream. When we got to the party, I tore the cake apart, made whipped cream, and got to layering everything in a deep bowl. I remembered someone telling me that if you melted vanilla ice cream, it was the perfect substitute for crème anglaise. Before you knew it, we had a perfect grocery store trifle. What's that saying . . . ? Necessity is the mother of invention—Well, here you go!

SERVES 10 TO 12

4 cups heavy cream

½ cup powdered sugar

½ teaspoon vanilla extract

1 store-bought chocolate Bundt cake

1 pint vanilla ice cream, melted

1 cup caramel sauce

1 cup chocolate sauce

1 cup Heath Bar toffee bits

2 Heath Bars, coarsely chopped (optional)

1. Using a stand mixer or hand mixer with the whisk attachment, mix the cream, sugar, and vanilla on low speed. As the cream thickens, increase the speed. Once it is thick and holds its form, stop mixing.

Chef Tip Never start the mixer on high when beating a liquid. Heavy cream is great unless it is covering your entire body and half of your kitchen!

2. To assemble the trifle, tear the cake into pieces. In a large glass bowl or trifle dish, layer about one-fifth of the cake pieces, whipped cream, melted ice cream, caramel sauce, chocolate sauce, toffee bits, and chopped Heath Bar pieces (if using). Continue layering four more times, ending with the toffee bits or Heath Bar pieces. (You can make this a day ahead, cover it, and refrigerate until you're ready to serve.

Celebrate,
celebrate, celebrate!

2

PARTY DAYS

These recipes are like your little black dress . . . they fit every occasion. They're always waiting and ready. They can be dressed up or down, but are always the talk of the party.

A few years after Luke and I got married, I decided to have a dinner party. I wanted to invite some of our friends and Luke's family to come over. On the menu were beef fillets cooked to order—for twenty-five people. Those of you who cook and entertain are probably rolling your eyes so far in the back of your heads they might get stuck! It's hard enough to get the temperature right for four steaks, much less twenty-five! Yes, I know. I know, I know!!! An hour before the party, I was in my daughter's room, in the middle of the floor, cleaning out her toy box—not showered, not dressed, and not a thing cooked. As guests arrived, I was a complete wreck.

I have gotten a lot better at cooking everything ahead of time these days. It didn't take me long to realize that our guests could care less what my daughter's toy box looks like. Yet I still get squirrelly before I host any party at my own house. No, it does not matter that I have owned my own catering company for twenty years. When I host my own parties, I am a woman possessed. Yes, I can give any other host helpful party prep advice: "No need to stress, these are friends coming to your house, not enemies," and "If the hostess is relaxed and fun, the party will be, too." and "The people make the party, not the perfectly pressed guest towels." Still, I lose my mind a touch whenever I host my own party. So do as I say, not as I do.

LEMON
Sparklers

————◈◈◈————

Specialty cocktails are a fun way to add an unforgettable detail to any party. This one is super simple, with only three ingredients. Served in champagne flutes or coupe glasses, it's elegant enough for fancy evening affairs but also couldn't be any more refreshing on a hot summer day.

SERVES 6

1 pint lemon sorbet

1 (750-milliliter) bottle limoncello

1 (750-milliliter) bottle Prosecco (don't break the bank; you are adding other things to it so it doesn't have to be the finest quality)

1. Spoon a scoop of sorbet the size of a melon ball into each glass. Add 1 ounce (2 tablespoons) limoncello. Top with Prosecco and serve.

Crabmeat Maison

———◇◇◇◇◇———

I love all the parties I cater but there are some that stand out in my mind. One in particular involved eighteen pounds of lump crabmeat—enough for 150 guests—and a silver punch bowl. Lord have mercy, that punch bowl full of Crabmeat Maison was a sight to behold, you want to talk about a showstopper! We did cheat just a bit, for a very good reason. We lined the bottom of the bowl with a gallon-size Ziploc bag full of ice. This ensured the outside of the bowl would frost from the cold ice, and also kept the crab nice and cold. Now, if you don't have 150 guests coming over and don't need eighteen pounds of crab, have no fear, there are lots of other fun ways to serve this delicate crab salad. I love to put it in butter lettuce wraps for a first course or a lovely luncheon. There is hardly anything better than this in a bowl with crostini or toast points. An endive leaf with a little crabmeat in it is also beautiful. And don't forget a shot glass with a cocktail fork, nothing wrong with that, either. It doesn't really matter how you choose to serve it—it's divine!

SERVES 4

½ cup mayonnaise

2 tablespoons finely chopped green onions (white and green parts)

1 tablespoon drained capers

Juice of ½ small lemon (about 1½ teaspoons)

½ teaspoon Creole seasoning (preferably Tony Chachere's)

1 pound lump crabmeat, picked well but gently to remove shell and cartilage and preserve the bulk of the lumps

1. In a small bowl, mix the mayonnaise, green onions, capers, lemon juice, and Creole seasoning. Add half of the sauce to the crabmeat in a medium bowl, mix gently, and evaluate. You only want enough sauce to moisten the crabmeat, not drown it. (This story is all about the crab, not the sauce.) If more sauce is needed, add it a spoonful at a time, being careful not to oversauce the crab. Cover and chill before serving.

HOT

HOT
Crawfish Dip

Until crawfish tails became readily available in frozen packages, this dip would have been impossible to make. I don't know about you, but if I am going to go through the trouble of peeling a crawfish I am damn sure going to eat the tail and not save it for later! The original version of this family recipe had a ton of red pepper in it, so much that you needed a gallon of beer to get through it. I substitute Creole seasoning, Tony Chachere's brand to be exact. When I cater a cocktail buffet, I always include at least one beautiful silver chafing dish, generally filled with a delicious, creamy dip. This one always gets rave reviews.

SERVES 20

2 pounds fresh or frozen peeled crawfish tails

½ cup sliced green onions (white and green parts)

8 tablespoons (1 stick) salted butter

3 (8-ounce) packages cream cheese, room temperature

8 cloves garlic, minced, or 2 teaspoons garlic powder

1 tablespoon Creole seasoning (preferably Tony Chachere's)

1½ teaspoons liquid crab boil

1½ teaspoons pepper

Salt

¼ to ½ cup chicken broth (if using fresh crawfish)

Assorted crackers, for serving

1. Thaw the crawfish in the package, if frozen; drain, reserving the liquid from the package.

2. In a large saucepan, cook the green onions in the butter until tender but not brown, about 3 minutes. Add the crawfish; cook over medium heat for about 4 minutes, until heated through. Break up any large pieces of crawfish.

3. Stir in the cream cheese, garlic, Creole seasoning, crab boil, pepper, and salt to taste. Stir in enough of the reserved crawfish liquid or chicken broth (if using fresh crawfish) until the mixture reaches dipping consistency. Cook until heated through. Serve warm with crackers.

Chef Tip When buying packaged crawfish tails always remember to look at the country of origin. You want to make sure they are from the U.S. Even if the name on the front says "Southern Crawfish Tails," still check the back. Chances are the only thing Southern about these tails is the name! Because there are no regulations for foreign crawfish, the quality can be unreliable—plus you'll be supporting American producers.

Smoked Salmon

SPREAD

I got this recipe from my daughters' friend Anna Barret when Anna was only fourteen years old! (My children have very sophisticated friends. Most kids at that age can barely make a peanut butter sandwich, much less whip up a to-die-for smoked salmon spread.) The key to this dip is to use hot-smoked salmon. When you purchase it at the store, it will look like a piece of grilled salmon, not the salmon you put on your bagel. I only use enough mayonnaise and cream cheese to bind the dip together. It's really about the salmon, so we don't want to hide that amazing flavor. Serve with your favorite cracker, crostini, or crudités.

SERVES 15 AS AN HORS D'OEUVRE

1 pound hot-smoked salmon

1 (8-ounce) package cream cheese, room temperature

½ cup mayonnaise

1½ tablespoons fresh lemon juice

2 tablespoons drained capers

1 tablespoon chopped fresh dill

⅓ cup finely chopped red onion

¼ cup finely chopped green onions (white and green parts)

1 teaspoon Creole seasoning (preferably Tony Chachere's)

1. Flake the smoked salmon with a fork and set it aside.

2. Mix the cream cheese with the mayonnaise in a large bowl until smooth. Add the lemon juice, capers, dill, red onion, green onions, and Creole seasoning and mix well. Fold in the smoked salmon, trying to keep as many flakes intact as possible.

3. Cover and chill for at least 2 hours before serving. (This can be made up to 3 days in advance.)

BRIE-STUFFED
Artichokes

I often wonder: Who was the brave soul who first tried an artichoke? Pretty sure there was no lemon drawn butter for dipping, yet this intrepid eater persisted. This recipe for stuffed artichokes was served at an engagement party I attended not long after Luke and I got married. It was simple, it was easy, it was delicious—so I stole it. Not the artichoke itself (I was raised better than that) but I damn sure stole the recipe. It is an unusual and unexpected addition to an antipasto platter or crudités tray and I could not love it any more. To eat it, your guests pull off each leaf and scrape the Brie and artichoke between their teeth. Make sure to put an extra bowl beside the tray of artichokes for the discarded leaves.

SERVES 20

3 or 4 medium artichokes

1 lemon

½ cup salt (for boiling the artichokes)

1 pound Brie, rind removed

1. Place the artichokes in a large pot of water, stem-side down. Cut the lemon in half, squeeze over the artichokes, and drop the squeezed lemon into the water. Add the salt to the water and bring to a boil. Cook the artichokes at a medium boil for 25 to 35 minutes. The artichokes are done when the outer leaves can be pulled off easily.

2. Drain the artichokes. Make sure you turn them upside down to let the excess water fall out.

3. Once they are cool enough to handle, pinch off a piece of the Brie and stuff it inside one of the outer leaves. Repeat, working from the outside in. Set aside while you stuff the remaining artichokes.

4. Just before serving, pop the artichokes in the microwave for about 30 seconds to melt the Brie. Serve immediately.

Chef Tip Once all the leaves have been pulled off, scrape the fuzzy, inedible part from the heart and cut the heart into pieces. Enjoy the fruit of all your labor!

SAUSAGE AND RED PEPPER
Stuffed Mushrooms

—◦◦◦◦◦—

When I'm writing catering menus, I am always looking for a one-bite, pick-up hors' d'oeuvre. I have stuffed mushrooms every which way but loose. Seriously, if it can fit in a mushroom cap, I have done it. Leek bread pudding, check. Oysters, check. Crawfish etouffee, check. Roasted veggies with Boursin cheese, check. Even with all these, this is the tried and true favorite that everyone loves. You can make them days ahead, they freeze beautifully, and are a breeze to put together. The filling is also an amazing dip on its own.

SERVES 15

30 nice-size white button mushrooms (big enough to stuff), plus 8 ounces mushrooms for the filling, sliced (about 3 cups)

1 pound bulk hot pork or Italian sausage

1 tablespoon canola oil

½ cup chopped onion

½ cup chopped red bell pepper

8 ounces cream cheese, room temperature

½ teaspoon Worcestershire sauce

Chef Tip If you want to make these ahead of time, store the unbaked stuffed mushrooms in an airtight container for up to 3 days in the refrigerator, or freeze them. If freezing, let them thaw overnight before baking.

1. Preheat the oven to 350°F. Brush the whole mushrooms with a clean, dry towel to remove any extra organic matter. Pull out and discard the stems and set the mushroom caps aside, stem-side up.

2. In a large skillet, brown the sausage, stirring often, for 8 to 10 minutes, until crumbled and no longer pink. Remove the sausage from the skillet with a slotted spoon and drain well. Wipe out the drippings from the skillet. In the same skillet, heat the oil and cook the sliced mushrooms, onion, and pepper until tender, 6 to 8 minutes. Stir together the cream cheese and Worcestershire sauce in a small bowl, then stir into the vegetable mixture. Add the cooked sausage. Heat and stir until the cheese is melted.

3. Stuff the sausage mixture into the mushroom caps. Place the caps on a rimmed baking sheet. Bake until the mushroom caps are tender, 15 to 20 minutes. Serve immediately.

TACKY TACKY
Meatballs

A fabulous invitation is your first opportunity to set the tone for your party. My friends Bob and Wilma Wilbanks understand this more than most: A few years back they threw the loveliest New Year's Day party. I will never forget when I opened the envelope of the invitation and the most beautiful glitter and sparkles came flooding out. I looked forward to this party for weeks. After an invitation like that, I could only imagine what the party would be like! Well, the sparkles and glitter were only the very tip of the iceberg. Amazing food, stunning flowers, and don't even get me started on the silver. Bob made these meatballs and served them in the most stunning, ornate silver chafing dish anyone has ever seen. I parked myself by the chafing dish and must have skewered ten pounds of meatballs. At one point, it looked like I was fishing. As embarrassing as my behavior was, I couldn't stop. I was addicted. This is the perfect holiday recipe. It can be made days ahead, is cooked in the slow cooker, has only four ingredients, and your guests will never forget it.

SERVES 25

1 (30- to 32-ounce) jar grape jelly

2 (12-ounce) bottles tomato-based chili sauce (preferably Heinz)

1 pinch cayenne pepper

5 pounds store-bought frozen cocktail meatballs

1. In a large bowl, combine the jelly, chili sauce, and cayenne pepper. Place the meatballs in a slow cooker, then pour the jelly mixture on top. Cover and cook on low for 3 to 4 hours, until the sauce has thickened. Serve immediately, or refrigerate in an airtight container for up to 4 days; reheat when you're ready to serve.

Chef Tip If you don't have a slow cooker, combine the jelly, chili sauce, and cayenne pepper in a Dutch oven or other large pot with a tight-fitting lid and cook over medium heat until the sauce is smooth, 10 to 12 minutes. Add the meatballs and bake in a 300°F oven for about 90 minutes.

THE PERFECT
Beef Tenderloin

I love it when my friends or family members go to a wedding that I didn't cater or help plan. I can hardly wait to hear all the details. The first question I always ask is: Was it a beef tenderloin, pork tenderloin, or chicken kind of wedding? Once I have that information, I can guess the answers to all the other questions. Beef tenderloin is expensive but very fabulous. It's hard to know just how many beef tenderloins my catering staff and I have cooked over the last twenty years. I have a feeling if we lined them up end to end they could circle the globe. Okay, maybe not, but I bet we could get from my house to the Mason-Dixon Line! I have to think so many of my clients choose it because it is universally loved and they want their guests to be wowed. Surely not because they want their guests to answer the next day that yes, indeed, it was a beef tenderloin wedding!

**SERVES 10 AS A PLATED DINNER,
20 AS PART OF A COCKTAIL BUFFET**

5 pounds beef tenderloin, cleaned, trimmed, and silverskin removed (you can ask your butcher to do this for you)

4 tablespoons (½ stick) salted butter, room temperature

1 tablespoon Worcestershire sauce

2 tablespoons salt

2 tablespoons pepper

Horseradish Mayonnaise (recipe follows), for serving

1. Preheat the oven to 500°F. Line a rimmed baking sheet with foil.

2. Place the beef tenderloin on the baking sheet. Rub with the butter, drizzle with the Worcestershire, and season with the salt and pepper on all sides. Tuck the tail of the tenderloin underneath to ensure the meat will cook evenly. (The tenderloin should look like a piece of cord wood, the same thickness from end to end.)

3. Open the oven door and quickly put the tenderloin inside. (The longer the door is open, the more heat will escape.) For a medium-rare tenderloin, cook for exactly 25 minutes, and for a rare tenderloin, cook for 22 minutes.

4. Remove from the oven and allow the meat to rest for 10 minutes before serving. (I know it is hard, but you have to let all the fibers in the meat reabsorb the juices. Otherwise all those juices will be on your cutting board, down your cabinet, and on your shoes instead of in your mouth!) Slice and serve with Horseradish Mayonnaise.

HORSERADISH MAYONNAISE

This simple sauce is the perfect complement to a beef tenderloin. Don't ever—and I mean ever—buy the store brand premade mess. It is a sad disappointment. You can make this in the time it takes you to park your car at the grocery store.

SERVES 4 TO 6

2 cups mayonnaise

1 (8-ounce) jar prepared horseradish, drained well

½ cup sour cream

2 teaspoons Worcestershire sauce

1 teaspoon Cajun seasoning

1 teaspoon pepper

Salt

1. Mix together the mayonnaise, horseradish, sour cream, Worcestershire, Cajun seasoning, pepper, and salt to taste in a small bowl. Cover and refrigerate until you're ready to serve. (You can make this up to 5 days in advance.)

RED ONION AND BASIL
Quesadillas

—◦◦◦◦◦—

The first job I ever had in the culinary world (after serving ice cream at the putt-putt golf and games) was at a catering company in Memphis, Tennessee, called Another Roadside Attraction. Another Roadside Attraction made these simple yet perfect quesadillas. We would grill them up, slice them like a pizza, and serve them as a passed hors d'oeuvre. At the parties we catered, I'd make one for the guest and one for me, one for the guest and one for me . . .

MAKES 24 HORS D'OEUVRES

8 flour tortillas

6 cups shredded muenster cheese

1 cup fresh basil chiffonade (see Chef Tip)

1 cup finely chopped red onion

8 tablespoons (1 stick) salted butter, cold

Chef Tip "Chiffonade" is a fancy term for leafy herbs or vegetables that are very finely cut. Stack fresh basil leaves and roll them lengthwise into a cigar. Now cut crosswise into thin strips. This method will ensure that your delicate basil does not bruise.

1. Lay out four of the tortillas on your counter. Divide the cheese between them. Sprinkle the basil and red onion on top of the cheese. Top with the remaining tortillas.

2. Hold the whole stick of butter and lightly rub it over the outside of the quesadillas on one side. Heat a griddle or skillet (preferably cast iron) over medium heat. Cooking in batches if necessary, place the quesadillas on the griddle, buttered-side down. Cook until the bottom tortilla is nice and crisp, 3 to 4 minutes. Butter the other tortilla (the one on top), flip, and cook until the second tortilla is crisp and the cheese is melted, another 3 to 4 minutes. Remove from the pan and cut each quesadilla into 6 wedges.

CHOCOLATE
Pots de Crème

——◦◦◦◦◦——

Chocolate pots de crème, now isn't that about the fanciest sounding dessert ever? I don't know about you, but any time I hear fancy French names for recipes, I panic. In my mind, fancy French means very hard, reserved for classically trained chefs. But let me tell you something. This recipe could not be any farther from tricky, technical, or intimidating. Literally three ingredients, a blender, and a fridge.

My grandmother left me the most beautiful demitasse cups. When we serve these pots de crème in her cups for Christmas, my heart literally sings. Now, you can serve the pots de crème in stemless martini glasses, ramekins, or shot glasses. All are stunning presentations.

One more bit of advice: There is always room for lagniappe—a Creole word for a little something extra—on this. Whipped cream, caramel sauce, fresh berries with mint, peppermint bark, or toffee bits would all be excellent.

SERVES 6

1 cup (6 ounces) semisweet chocolate chips

2 large eggs

⅔ cup light cream, heated just to boiling

1. In the jar of a blender, combine the chocolate, eggs, and cream. Cover and blend on high speed for about 3 minutes, until the chocolate chips are completely melted.

2. Pour into six 4-ounce demitasse cups or 6-ounce custard cups. Refrigerate, covered, for at least 4 hours before serving.

DAY-AFTER-PARTY
Egg Casserole

I love the day after a party almost as much as I love the night of the party. Your house is still clean, the flowers are still fresh, and the "good company" soap in the bathroom has hardly been used! And you're still smiling remembering the sight of all your closest friends in the same room laughing and having a ball. Don't forget all the leftovers! We always do a charcuterie and cheese platter for parties, and although all my guests enjoy it, I always overdo it and have lots and lots of meats and cheeses left over. This casserole is a wonderful way to use all that yummy goodness and keep the party going.

SERVES 8

8 slices white sandwich bread, crusts removed

2½ cups chopped leftover charcuterie (prosciutto, salami, etc.)

3 cups chopped, grated, and/or crumbled leftover cheese (Brie, goat, blue, etc.)

½ cup chopped olives

1 cup chopped sun-dried tomatoes, roasted red peppers, artichoke hearts, or a combination

2 cups milk

10 large eggs

1 tablespoon Creole seasoning (preferably Tony Chachere's)

2 teaspoons Worcestershire sauce

2 teaspoons kosher salt

1 teaspoon pepper

1. Cut four of the bread slices on the diagonal into four triangles each; cut the remaining bread into cubes. Lightly grease a 9 x 13-inch baking dish. Arrange the bread triangles to cover the bottom. Top with the bread cubes. Top with the charcuterie, cheese, olives, and sun-dried tomatoes.

2. In a bowl, whisk together the milk, eggs, Creole seasoning, Worcestershire, salt, and pepper.

3. Pour the egg mixture over the cheese and charcuterie. Cover and let sit in the fridge for at least 1 hour or overnight.

4. Preheat the oven to 375°F. Let the casserole stand at room temperature for about 10 minutes.

5. Bake the casserole until the middle is set and the top is lightly browned, about 50 minutes.

The Delta isn't a place easily explained. It must be experienced.

3

DELTA DAYS

All soft drinks are called Coke where I come from. If you want a Sprite, ask for a Coke. If you want a Diet Coke, ask for a Coke. If you want a root beer, ask for a Coke. No, it doesn't make much sense, but neither does the Delta.

The Mississippi Delta is often referred to as the most Southern place (in the below-the-Mason-Dixon-line sense of the word) on Earth. People, this doesn't even begin to describe it. The Delta is a place of juxtapositions. Some the best authors of the twentieth century hail from the region, yet it has the highest rates of illiteracy in America.

It boasts some of the most beautiful antebellum homes in existence, but across from those grand columned homes, you will see the most meager houses without indoor plumbing, even today. The Delta isn't a place easily explained. It must be experienced. Once you do, it gets in you and never leaves. It's a soulful place. These are the recipes that transport me to the middle of the Delta flatlands where history, culture, food, and fun go hand in hand and every day is a celebration.

MASON JAR COCKTAILS

Packing a cooler is something that I learned to do at a very young age. Daddy always looked for teaching moments. If he was mixing a drink, the tutorial began. Loading charcoal into the barbecue pit, time for more instruction. Packing a cooler for a boat ride down the river, step-by-step lesson learning. These mason jar cocktails were not a part of his lesson plan, but I know he will approve. Cocktails are hard to mix on a boat, or the sandbar for that matter. Mix your cocktails up, pour into mason jars, and throw them in the cooler. They fit nicely with your beer and snacks. I like to make at least three different cocktails: one with vodka, one with gin, and one with tequila.

Delta Dawn

SERVES 4

4 ounces (½ cup) vodka
(I like Cathead brand)

2 ounces (¼ cup) elderflower
liqueur (such as St-Germain)

2 ounces (¼ cup) white
cranberry juice

2 ounces (¼ cup) fresh
lemon juice

1. Mix all the ingredients in a pint-size wide-mouth mason jar. Screw the lid on tight and pack in the cooler or put in the fridge to chill until you're ready to serve. Divide into jars or glasses to serve.

River Rat

SERVES 1

2 ounces (¼ cup) tequila

1½ cups fresh ruby red
grapefruit juice

1 tablespoon honey

1 teaspoon fresh lime juice

1. Mix all the ingredients in a pint-size wide-mouth mason jar. Screw the lid on tight and pack in the cooler or put in the fridge to chill until you're ready to serve.

Blues Boy

MAKES 3

1 (12-ounce) container
blackberries

2 tablespoons sugar

1½ ounces
(3 tablespoons) fresh
lime juice

6 ounces (¾ cup) gin

15 mint leaves, torn

1½ cups seltzer water

1. Puree the berries and sugar in a food processor. Strain the puree and discard the seeds. You should have about 1 cup puree.

2. Put one-third of the puree, 1 tablespoon of the lime juice, 2 ounces of the gin, and one-third of the torn mint leaves into each of three pint-size wide-mouth mason jars. Just before serving, top off with ½ cup seltzer each.

3. Screw the lids on tight and pack in the cooler or put in the fridge to chill until you're ready to serve.

BIRTHPLACE OF THE BLUES?

The precise origins of the blues are lost to time, but one of the primal centers for the music in Mississippi was Dockery Farms. For nearly three decades the plantation was intermittently the home of Charley Patton (c. 1891-1934), the most important early Delta blues musician. Patton himself learned from fellow Dockery resident Henry Sloan and influenced many other musicians who came here, including Howlin' Wolf, Willie Brown, Tommy Johnson, and Roebuck "Pops" Staples.

FRIED
Pork Chops

One of my best friends, Cordilla, once described a meal she had cooked the night before—fried pork chops, fried green tomatoes, fried hushpuppies—and at the end of her elaborate, detailed description she said, "Honey, if it ain't fried, we don't want it!" This method of frying will ensure moist and tender pork chops every time.

SERVES 8

1½ cups all-purpose flour

1¼ teaspoons salt

1¼ teaspoons pepper

1 teaspoon Cajun seasoning

1 teaspoon garlic powder

1 cup cold buttermilk

8 (8-ounce) bone-in pork chops (about 1 inch thick)

4 cups peanut oil

Chef Tip When facing the choice of bone or no bone, always choose the bone. Bone-in meats will be more moist and flavorful.

1. In a shallow bowl or rimmed plate, combine the flour, salt, pepper, Cajun seasoning, and garlic powder and mix well. Pour the buttermilk into another shallow bowl. One at a time, place the pork chops in the buttermilk and turn to coat. Remove the pork chop from the buttermilk and dredge both sides in the flour. Shake off any excess flour and set the chop aside on a platter. Repeat with the remaining chops.

2. Heat the oil in a deep-fat fryer or large heavy-bottomed pot to 350°F. Line a large plate with paper towels.

3. Drop the pork chops into the oil. Fry for about 8 minutes total, turning once about halfway through, until golden brown.

4. Remove the chops from the oil and drain on the paper towels. Serve immediately.

Chef Tip After frying, let the oil cool, strain it, and store in an airtight container in the pantry for the next time you are frying. However, if you are frying fish, the fishy smell can penetrate the oil. If you want to reuse that oil to fry something else, cut a potato into four large wedges and place in the hot oil. The potato will absorb the fishy flavor and you can proceed with frying.

Mississippi Caviar Dip

I can still remember my first time trying caviar like it was yesterday. I was eight years old, and we were in Laurel, Mississippi, for my new cousin's christening. My aunt Joy, who was not only an amazing cook but also one of my favorite people on the planet, had prepared all the food for the luncheon after the church service. Momma kept talking about how they had fresh caviar flown in for this special occasion. (The Piggly Wiggly in Laurel doesn't stock beluga caviar.) At the luncheon, Aunt Joy had the caviar mounded atop a cake of lemon-zest cream cheese—it was as big as the bottom tier of a wedding cake—on a silver platter. I couldn't wait to try all those tiny black pearls. But one bite and I almost threw up in my mouth—I was totally overwhelmed by the saltiness, not to mention the slime factor. Tears started running down my cheeks, my face got flushed, but standing around that dining room table with all those lovely people, I had no choice but to swallow. It was only many years later that I repaired my relationship with those tiny black pearls. In the South, black-eyed peas are another kind of "caviar," and this dip is much less expensive and more readily available in Mississippi. I prefer to use leftover black-eyed peas over the canned ones but if you are in a hurry, canned will do in a pinch.

SERVES 10 TO 12

4 cups cooked black-eyed peas or
2 (15-ounce) cans, drained

½ red, orange, or yellow bell pepper, finely chopped (about ½ cup)

½ medium onion, finely chopped (about ½ cup)

4 slices bacon, cooked and chopped (reserve the grease for another use)

½ cup chopped drained canned artichoke hearts

½ cup chow chow or pepper jelly

¾ cup Disappearing Vinaigrette (page 212)

Salt and pepper

Tortilla chips, for serving

1. Combine the black-eyed peas, bell pepper, onion, bacon, artichoke hearts, chow chow, and vinaigrette in a large bowl. Season with salt and pepper to taste. Cover and refrigerate for a few hours (or up to 2 days) to chill and so the flavors can combine.

2. Serve with tortilla chips.

Mom Tip This also makes a great side dish or topping for hamburgers or hotdogs.

Pocketknife Slaw

Every Southern girl thinks her daddy is the most intelligent, funniest, most talented, and most special. I am no exception. There is hardly anything my daddy can't do, and to top it all off he is an amazing cook. Our friends are always clamoring for him to make this slaw when we have a get-together. I know exactly what you are thinking: Slaw? Who gives a damn about slaw! Slaw is just an afterthought. Well, not his! It's quite spectacular—just ask the man himself! The cabbage doesn't have to be cut perfectly—you could even use a pocketknife if that is all you have!

SERVES 6

1 head green cabbage

3 cups mayonnaise

1 tablespoon yellow mustard

Juice of 1 lemon

1 ripe tomato, diced

Salt and pepper

1. Cut the cabbage into quarters and cut out the core. Thinly slice the cabbage crosswise. Place the cabbage in a large bowl. Spoon the mayonnaise into the middle of the cabbage. Spoon the mustard on top of the mayo. Then squeeze the lemon over the mayonnaise. (This way all the seeds from the lemon will get caught on top of the mayo, making it a breeze to remove them. Otherwise, they will fall under the cabbage and you will have a fishing expedition on your hands, one that doesn't end with sunshine or a cold beer, just a lot of aggravation.)

2. Pick off any lemon seeds. Mix the mayo, mustard, lemon juice, and cabbage. Add the tomato and gently toss. Taste and add a generous amount of salt and pepper. Serve immediately.

3. If you want to make this ahead, you can mix the mayo, mustard, and lemon juice dressing in an airtight container. Place the shredded cabbage in a Ziploc bag. Store them both in the fridge. This can be done a few days ahead of time. Then when you are ready to serve, you just toss all the ingredients together.

MARTHA'S

MARTHA'S
Deviled Eggs

You say to-may-to and I say to-mah-to. You say stuffed eggs, I say deviled eggs. The Delta is split down the middle on stuffed eggs versus deviled eggs. I say deviled, but my friend Miss Martha Gillis—a lovely cook, friend, mother, and hostess—says stuffed. Now, I am guilty of overusing certain words—for example, the word "lovely." I use it to describe a sunset, a flower arrangement, an invitation. But Martha is someone who is truly lovely. This is her deviled egg recipe and it is just, well, lovely! Deviled eggs are one of the world's most perfect foods. And I think my recipe is pretty damn good! But Martha's recipe is lovelier.

SERVES 12

1 dozen large eggs, room temperature

½ cup mayonnaise

4 teaspoons yellow mustard

1 tablespoon sweet pickle relish, plus 1 teaspoon relish juice

Salt and pepper

Sliced green olives, for garnish

1. Bring a large pot of water to a boil. Add the eggs and boil for about 15 minutes.

2. Drain the eggs in a colander in the sink and run cold water over them to cool them quickly.

3. Peel the eggs and slice them in half lengthwise. Remove the yolks and place them in a bowl, reserving the egg whites on platters.

4. Mash the egg yolks with a fork until smooth. Add the mayo, mustard, relish, and relish juice and stir to blend. Add salt and pepper to taste.

5. Transfer the yolk mixture to a Ziploc bag and zip it closed. Cut a small hole in one of the bottom corners of the bag. Squeeze the yolk mixture through the hole into the egg whites.

6. Top with sliced olives. Place in the fridge until you're ready to serve, up to 1 hour.

COUNTRY CLUB
Potatoes

During the 1930s, the government implemented the WPA program. It was a way to put unskilled workers to work, building roads and other municipal buildings to help with unemployment and to improve communities. In Rosedale, where I grew up, they decided to use the program to build a country club, complete with a golf course and swimming pool. This is where we lived in the summertime and it was heaven on earth. Miss Anna Mea ran the snack bar and we had a charge account. Momma would drop us off and we would eat all the Popsicles, Nabs, Nutter Butters, and Now and Laters we could stand. But the country club didn't have a restaurant, so most functions there were potlucks. These cheesy potatoes were always on the buffet.

SERVES 8 TO 10

8 medium baking potatoes, well scrubbed

8 tablespoons (1 stick) salted butter

1 bunch green onions, chopped (white and green parts)

2 cups shredded cheddar cheese

16 ounces sour cream

8 ounces cream cheese, room temperature

½ cup milk, plus more if needed

1 teaspoon salt, or more to taste

½ teaspoon pepper

½ teaspoon paprika

Finely chopped fresh chives, for garnish

1. Preheat the oven to 400°F. Pierce each potato with a fork in a few places so they won't explode. Bake the potatoes until tender, 30 to 45 minutes. Remove from the oven and turn the oven down to 350°F. When cool enough to handle, scoop out the insides into a large bowl (discard the peels) and mash coarsely.

2. Melt the butter in a skillet. Add the green onions and sauté for 3 to 4 minutes, until tender. To the bowl with the potatoes, add 1 cup of the cheddar cheese, the sour cream, cream cheese, cooked green onions, milk, salt, pepper, and paprika. Stir well. Taste and adjust the spices; adjust the consistency with more milk if needed.

3. Pour the mixture into a 9 x 13-inch baking dish. Bake at 350°F for 30 minutes, until warmed through.

4. Top with the remaining cheese and the chives. Return to the oven for a few more minutes, until the cheese is melted and bubbly. Serve immediately.

MOON PIE
Ice Cream Sandwiches

To me Moon Pies are one of the most perfect foods known to man. Marshmallows, graham crackers, and chocolate—what else could you want? Except maybe a scoop of ice cream!

SERVES 6

6 Moon Pies (any flavor you love)

½ gallon of your favorite ice cream, softened

1. Split each Moon Pie in half like a hamburger bun. Place a scoop of ice cream on the bottom and top with the other half of the Moon Pie. Wrap in plastic wrap and place in the freezer until the ice cream has had a chance to harden and you are ready to serve, at least 4 hours.

JALAPEÑO PIMENTO CHEESE ON
Cornbread Muffins

I just cannot imagine writing a cookbook without a pimento cheese recipe, so I've included one in all three of my cookbooks. This version adds pickled jalapeños and a little bit of the juice to give it an extra kick. There is hardly any other way to serve pimento cheese except on a saltine cracker, but sometimes you just get in a mood for something different. These little cornbread muffins come together super quickly and freeze beautifully. Split the muffins in half and fill them with the pimento cheese. You can serve them room temperature or heat them in the oven just until the cheese starts to melt if you want to make this hors d'oeuvre unforgettable! It wouldn't hurt my feelings if you topped them with a little bacon as well.

JALAPEÑO PIMENTO CHEESE

MAKES 2 CUPS

1 (8-ounce) block white cheddar cheese, shredded (about 2 cups)

1 cup mayonnaise

2 ounces parmesan cheese, shredded (about ½ cup)

¾ cup roasted red bell peppers (half a 12-ounce jar), drained and diced

¼ cup chopped drained pickled jalapeños, plus 2 teaspoons juice from the jalapeños

¼ cup chopped green onions (white and green parts)

¼ teaspoon hot sauce

¼ teaspoon Creole seasoning (preferably Tony Chachere's)

¼ teaspoon Worcestershire sauce

1. Stir together the cheddar, mayonnaise, parmesan, red peppers, jalapeños, jalapeño juice, green onions, hot sauce, Creole seasoning, and Worcestershire in a large bowl. Cover and store in the refrigerator until you're ready to serve, up to 10 days.

CORNBREAD MUFFINS

MAKES 24 REGULAR-SIZE MUFFINS OR 72 MINI MUFFINS

2 cups self-rising flour

2 cups self-rising white cornmeal

1 teaspoon sugar

2 large eggs

3 cups buttermilk

24 tablespoons (1½ cups) vegetable oil, for the muffin tin

1. Preheat the oven to 400°F. Mix the flour, cornmeal, and sugar in one bowl. In another bowl, whisk the eggs with the buttermilk. Add the dry ingredients to the wet ingredients and mix until smooth.

2. Pour 1 tablespoon oil into each cup of two regular muffin pans or 1 teaspoon into each mini muffin cup. Heat the muffin pans in the oven for 5 to 7 minutes. Carefully pour the hot oil onto the cornbread mixture. Stir well.

3. Pour the batter into the muffin cups and bake until golden brown, about 25 minutes (or about 20 minutes for mini muffins). Serve immediately. To freeze for later, let cool to room temperature and then freeze in an airtight container for up to 6 months. Thaw overnight in the refrigerator and then reheat in a 350° oven until warm, about 20 minutes.

SKILLET CORNBREAD

To make the cornbread in a skillet instead of as muffins: Decrease the oil to ¼ cup. Pour the oil into an 8-inch cast-iron (or other ovenproof) skillet. Heat the skillet in the oven for 5 to 7 minutes. Carefully pour the oil from the skillet into the batter and stir well. Pour the batter into the skillet and bake until browned, about 25 minutes.

Beulah Ribs

Edmond Young ran a small grocery store in Beulah, Mississippi. Like so many other Chinese Americans, his parents had migrated to Mississippi. They came to work in the cotton fields as laborers. Many quickly began opening small grocery stores in African American neighborhoods. When Daddy would load us in the car to take us from Rosedale to our family farm in Beulah, we were beyond thrilled. My favorite part of those days was going to Edmond's store to get lunch. He had a spectacular meat counter that had everything from pickled pigs' feet to bologna.

Edmond would see us coming and start making the sandwiches: Wonder Bread, yellow mustard, and BBQ ham. I would watch through the glass of the meat counter as he would wrap each one in wax paper. The small, rickety table with plastic chairs nearby was always crowded with the Young family, the table piled high with the most interesting food I have ever seen. Bowls of steaming noodles, mounds of greens, fried rice, delicate soft dumplings, and a rack of ribs, black as night. It wasn't until many years later that I was able to taste those amazing ribs, when Daddy had a party and Edmond brought his Chinese ribs. I liked to die they were so divine. Daddy asked many times for him to give us the sauce recipe. Edmond would always reply, "Just call me when you want some BBQ sauce and I will make it for you." This was his way of saying you don't have a snowball's chance in hell of getting the recipe.

Years later, I had worked my way into a rib contest with Luke's BFF, Bernard, and I needed a ringer, so I took Edmond up on his offer and had Daddy order a jar of sauce for me. When I went to the grocery to pick it up, I was early and it wasn't ready yet. Edmond quickly went behind the meat counter to make his secret recipe. Well, I used my old spying technique and peered through the meat counter. I watched him mix half KC Masterpiece BBQ sauce, and half hoisin sauce. That was his secret recipe! My recipe is inspired by that idea, but is unlike any store-bought sauce.

SERVES 6 TO 8

½ cup soy sauce

½ cup hoisin sauce

½ cup ketchup

6 tablespoons dry sherry

3 tablespoons dark brown sugar

6 cloves garlic, minced

1 tablespoon grated peeled fresh ginger

6 tablespoons honey

2 racks spare ribs (about 2 pounds each)

1 tablespoon seasoned salt

1. Preheat the oven to 275°F.

2. To make the BBQ sauce, in a small saucepan combine the soy sauce, hoisin, ketchup, sherry, brown sugar, garlic, ginger, and honey. Bring to a boil over medium-high heat. Turn the heat off. Set aside 1 cup of the sauce.

3. Place the ribs side by side on a very large sheet of foil. Rub the seasoned salt on the front and back sides of the ribs. Brush the remaining sauce onto the ribs. Wrap the ribs tightly in the foil, making sure no steam can escape and transfer the ribs to a baking sheet.

4. Bake the ribs for 2 hours or until they are tender.

5. Preheat the grill to medium heat.

6. Unwrap the ribs and place them on the grill. Grill the ribs for about 10 minutes; after about 5 minutes, turn the ribs and baste with the reserved sauce to caramelize the sauce on the ribs.

7. Let the ribs rest for 10 to 15 minutes, then serve.

Bumper crops of
fruits and vegetables
are at their best this
time of year

—◇◇◇ 4 ◇◇◇—

SUMMER DAYS

Summer in the Mississippi Delta is as hot as the hinges of hell. Brace yourself, settle in, and celebrate!

I can remember waiting for summer all year long as a kid. The long days of winter seemed to drone on and on. Homework, teachers, structure, and alarms be damned! I pined for the free-and-easy days of summertime. Even though my school days are well behind me, I still long for summer. The structure of life naturally relaxes then and so does my cooking. These recipes are simple yet satisfying. Bumper crops of fruits and vegetables are at their best this time of year, so that means that your cooking doesn't have to be over the top or difficult. Let the abundance of great ingredients do the impressing.

WATERMELON AND TOMATO
Gazpacho

Watermelon and tomatoes in cold soup!? I get it. It seems like a strange combination until you remember that a tomato is really a fruit. I don't know about you, but I have sure had some ripe tomatoes as sweet as a Jolly Rancher candy. But do not even think about making this unless watermelons and tomatoes are at their peak season. Otherwise, it's a big waste of time and a huge disappointment.

When I make this soup, I prefer to keep it pretty chunky. Just a few pulses in the food processor and I am done. If you prefer, you can process the hell out of it and then push it through a fine-mesh strainer. This produces a more refined and elegant presentation. Add a little dollop of crabmeat or cold boiled shrimp and buddy, you have got one showstopper on your hands.

**SERVES 4 AS A MAIN COURSE,
8 AS A FIRST COURSE**

3 ripe tomatoes, peeled (see Chef Tip) and quartered

3 cups seedless watermelon chunks

¾ cup V8 or vegetable juice cocktail

½ cup chopped yellow onion

½ cup chopped green bell pepper

¼ cup chopped peeled and seeded cucumber

1 clove garlic, peeled

2 tablespoons olive oil

2 tablespoons fresh lemon juice

2 teaspoons salt

¼ teaspoon ground white pepper

⅛ teaspoon Tabasco sauce or hot sauce

1 teaspoon Worcestershire sauce

1. Place all the ingredients in a food processor. Process just a little if you want a chunky soup. If you prefer, pulse until smooth and then pour the soup through a fine-mesh strainer for a more delicate soup without pulp. Cover and chill before serving.

Chef Tip This will make peeling the tomatoes super easy: Cut an *X* on the flower end of a tomato, just piercing the skin. Drop the tomato in boiling water for 1 minute; remove and place in an ice bath. Remove from the ice water and use a paring knife to peel off the skin.

WHITE PEACH

WHITE PEACH
Sangria

———◦◦◇◇◇◦◦———

I am a beer girl through and through. When I am lucky enough to get invited to very fancy wine dinners, where each course is paired with a different, amazing wine, I bring cold beer in my purse and drink in the bathroom at these lovely affairs! But every now and then I will veer off of the beer train if I have a really good reason to. Like this white peach sangria. For this recipe, make sure you find really ripe, juicy peaches.

SERVES 4 TO 6

1 bottle (750 milliliters) dry white wine

¾ cup peach-flavored vodka

6 tablespoons frozen lemonade concentrate, thawed

¼ cup sugar

1 pound white peaches, pitted and sliced

¾ cup seedless red grapes, halved, or 1 red apple, roughly chopped

¾ cup seedless green grapes, halved, or 1 green apple, roughly chopped

1. In a large pitcher, combine the wine, vodka, lemonade concentrate, and sugar. Stir until the sugar is dissolved. Add the peaches and the red and green grapes. Refrigerate the sangria until well chilled, at least 2 hours or overnight, to blend the flavors.

2. Serve over ice, and use a slotted spoon to include peach slices and grapes in each serving.

Fig
PRESERVES

———◆◇◆———

My grandmother is the best cook and homemaker I have ever met. When my brothers and I would come to spend weekends in the summer, she would stay in the kitchen making petite homemade biscuits, fig jam, and beautiful cakes. This was how she showed her love. On the side of her home, she had giant fig trees. Every morning she would get up early, pick the figs, and then carefully wash them. Then she would stand at the sink in her nightgown and peel each tiny fruit. After dividing them between us, she would pour cold heavy cream over them. In case you didn't know, peeling figs takes the patience of Job and lots of love. If anyone ever peels a fig for you there is only one reason: They love you deeply. The good news is you don't have to peel the figs for this recipe.

This is without a doubt the most beautiful jar of preserves you will put up all year. The figs look like glass jewels in the jar. What a glorious sight in the middle of January when you are longing for a taste of summer.

MAKES 8 HALF-PINT JARS

2 teaspoons baking soda

5 cups fresh figs (about 2 pounds)

1½ cups sugar

5 tablespoons salted butter

1 teaspoon vanilla extract

1 lemon, thinly sliced into rounds, seeds removed

1 tablespoon fresh lemon juice

1½ teaspoons ground cinnamon

1 teaspoon grated peeled fresh ginger

½ teaspoon ground cloves

1 pinch salt

1. In a large bowl, dissolve the baking soda in about 2 quarts water. Immerse the figs in the water. Gently stir to wash the figs, then drain off the water and rinse the figs thoroughly with cool fresh water.

2. Place the figs in a large, heavy-bottomed pot. Add 1 cup water, the sugar, butter, vanilla, lemon slices, lemon juice, cinnamon, ginger, and cloves. Stir very gently, making sure to keep the figs whole and intact.

3. Bring to a boil over medium heat. Reduce the heat to a simmer. Cook until the figs are golden brown and coated in syrup, about 1 hour. Stir very gently from time to time to ensure the figs do not burn on the bottom. Add the salt.

4. Meanwhile, sterilize eight ½-pint jars and their lids and rings by boiling them for 10 minutes. Briefly drain the jars upside down on a clean kitchen towel on the counter.

5. Pack the figs into the hot sterilized jars. Top them off with syrup until the jars are filled to about ¼ inch from the top. Wipe the rims of the jars, top with lids, and screw on the rings.

6. Fill a large stockpot halfway with water, enough to fully cover the jars by at least 1 inch, and bring to a boil over high heat. Carefully lower the jars into the water. Bring the water back to a full boil and boil for 15 minutes.

7. Remove the jars from the pot and place them on the counter to cool. The lids will pop as they begin to seal. When cool, store the jars in the pantry. (If the lids do not pop, you must store the jars in the refrigerator.) Wait at least 3 days before opening the jars. Once opened, the jam can be stored in the refrigerator for up to 2 weeks.

MOMMA'S
Bread and Butter Pickles

According to my mother's cousin Caroline, on the day I was born Momma was putting up bread and butter pickles. I was a week and a half late and she was just beside herself. When my great-grandmother called to check on Momma, she exclaimed, "Sheila, you're doing what!? You need to be resting!" Momma quickly replied, "I need to be putting up pickles." A couple hours after the last jar was done she went into labor. I have always loved bread and butter pickles, and canning for that matter, and that must be the reason why.

MAKES ABOUT 2 QUARTS

5½ cups thinly sliced pickling cucumbers
(about 1½ pounds)

1½ tablespoons kosher salt

1 cup thinly sliced onion (about 1 onion)

1 cup sugar

1 cup white vinegar

½ cup apple cider vinegar

¼ cup packed brown sugar

1½ teaspoons mustard seeds

½ teaspoon celery seeds

⅛ teaspoon ground turmeric

1. Combine the cucumbers and salt in a large bowl. Cover and refrigerate for 1½ hours.

2. Drain the cucumbers in a colander in the sink, rinse in cold water, then drain again and return to the bowl. Add the onion to the cucumbers.

3. Combine the sugar, white vinegar, cider vinegar, brown sugar, mustard seeds, celery seeds, and turmeric in a medium saucepan. Bring to a simmer over medium heat, stirring until the sugar dissolves. Pour the hot vinegar mixture over the cucumbers and onion and let stand at room temperature for 1 hour, until completely cooled. Cover and refrigerate for 24 hours. Store in an airtight container in the refrigerator for up to 2 weeks.

Tomato Pie

———◦◇◇◇◦———

I can't talk tomato pie without telling you the mother of all tomato stories. When my husband, Luke, and I started our vegetable farm, we had a very clear plan: He would grow the vegetables and I would sell them. So Luke planted 10,000 tomato plants, and a few months later I got in our used prison van and headed to Memphis to sell those tomatoes. When I wasn't out trying to sell the tomatoes, I was cooking up everything I could think of with tomatoes. When I wasn't dreaming up tomato recipes, I was canning tomatoes. When I wasn't canning tomatoes, I was drinking vodka . . . straight! (If you have never been faced with 4,000 pounds of tomatoes and no place to take them, then you don't know real terror.) I was on my porch with a glass of vodka in my hand when Luke walked by and said, "Some people like to add ice and Bloody Mary mix to their vodka, Elizabeth." And that, good people, is how my company Debutante Farmer Bloody Mary Mix was born.

In addition to Bloody Mary mix, during tomato season I make this pie almost daily. It comes together in a snap and is perfectly portable, and your guests and friends will always leave asking for the recipe.

SERVES 6

4 heirloom tomatoes, sliced (or any good ripe tomatoes will work; about 4 pounds)

Salt and pepper

10 basil leaves, cut in chiffonade (see Chef Tip, page 79)

1 cup mayonnaise

1 cup shredded mozzarella cheese

1 cup shredded parmesan cheese

4 ounces goat cheese, crumbled (½ cup)

1 (9-inch) pie crust, fully baked

1. Preheat the oven to 350°F.

2. Place the tomatoes in a colander in the sink and generously salt them. Let them drain for 15 minutes. Remove from the colander and pat dry with paper towels.

3. In a medium bowl, mix the mayonnaise, mozzarella, and parmesan.

4. Layer half the tomatoes and all the basil and goat cheese in the pie crust. Sprinkle with salt and pepper and then finish layering with the rest of the tomatoes. Top with the mayonnaise mixture and spread it evenly, completely covering the tomatoes.

5. Bake until lightly browned, about 20 minutes. Serve immediately.

FRIED GREEN TOMATOES

It has been said that if you deep-fried a stick it would taste pretty good! I have never tried it but I have fried green tomatoes and served them topped with just about everything imaginable. Here's how to make them: Slice green (unripe) tomatoes ½ inch thick. Place them in a shallow dish, cover with buttermilk, and refrigerate for 1 hour. In a shallow bowl or plate, mix some cornmeal, seasoned salt, Cajun seasoning, and black pepper. Remove the tomatoes from the buttermilk, shaking off any excess. Dredge in the cornmeal mixture and deep-fry in 350°F oil until they are golden brown and float to the top of the pot, about 6 minutes. Drain briefly on paper towels and serve hot.

Let your mind go wild for toppings. I can hardly think of anything that would not be good atop a hot, crisp fried green tomato. Here are a few of my favorite toppings:

- lump crabmeat
- pepper jelly
- pimento cheese
- shrimp remoulade
- bacon jam
- ranch dressing
- egg salad

COLD
Cucumber Dip

—◦◦◦◦◦—

I know you have all had that experience in a store when you pick up a dress that doesn't look like much on the hanger but is a knockout when you try it on. This recipe is the equivalent of that dress. You might look at the title and be tempted to turn the page. But I beg you to try this knockout. Of course, this dip can be enjoyed with crostini and crudités, but that's only the beginning. It is also amazing with lamb or cold poached salmon. I have even put it on hamburgers and hotdogs at a simple cookout.

Now, there is one key tip to this recipe. You must get as much of the juice out of the cucumber as humanly possible. Otherwise you will end up with a watery mess.

SERVES 6

1½ pounds cucumbers, peeled, cut In half lengthwise, seeds removed

Salt and pepper

¾ cup sour cream

¾ cup plain Greek yogurt

¼ cup mayonnaise

3 tablespoons chopped dill

1 tablespoon fresh lemon juice

2 teaspoons minced garlic

2 teaspoons champagne vinegar

1. Using a food processor, puree the cucumbers. Line a colander with a cheesecloth and set it in the sink. Mix 1½ teaspoons salt with the cucumber puree and transfer it to the colander. Let sit and drain for 1 hour.

2. Gather the cheesecloth together and give the cucumber one more good squeeze to ensure it's as dry as possible.

3. Place the cucumber pulp in a bowl and add the sour cream, yogurt, mayonnaise, dill, lemon juice, garlic, vinegar, and ⅛ teaspoon pepper. Mix well.

4. Add more salt and pepper to taste. Cover and refrigerate until chilled thoroughly, at least 2 hours or up to 4 days, before serving.

JUST RIGHT
Squash Casserole

—◇◇◇◇◇—

A plot of squash that is half the size of a football field yields a ton of squash. No joke, a literal ton of squash. When my husband and I first started the farm, we did everything in the world I could think of to use all the squash. Squash hushpuppies, squash bread, squash pickles; we froze the squash and even gave squash to the girls to make dolls and little animals out of. We were desperate. We were scared to sleep at night because when you slept, the squash grew. When we would visit friends, I would bring crates of squash with me. We didn't get invited back. When I started bringing this squash casserole instead, everything changed. We couldn't get invited back quick enough! Squash all by its lonesome has a very high water content and doesn't really have a ton of flavor. But casseroles are all about the goo! The cheese and cream sauce are the stars of this show, and the squash very happily takes the back seat.

SERVES 10

3 pounds yellow squash, sliced

½ onion, thinly sliced (about ½ cup)

12 tablespoons (1½ sticks) salted butter

½ cup all-purpose flour

2 cups milk, hot

1½ cups shredded cheddar cheese

½ cup shredded parmesan cheese

Salt and pepper

2 large eggs, beaten

20 butter crackers (such as Ritz or Keebler Club or Town House), crushed

1. Preheat the oven to 350°F.

2. In a pot, boil the squash and onion in water to cover until just tender, about 12 minutes. Drain in a colander in the sink and press the vegetables to extract as much liquid as possible.

3. Melt 8 tablespoons (1 stick) of the butter in a small skillet. Add the flour and stir until smooth. Add the milk gradually, whisking constantly. Once the mixture gets hot, after about 5 minutes, it will thicken; it should be thick enough to coat the back of a spoon. Remove from the heat.

4. In a large bowl, combine the drained squash and onion, sauce, cheddar, parmesan, and salt and pepper to taste. Mix in the eggs. Pour into a 9 x 13-inch glass baking dish. Cut the remaining 4 tablespoons butter into six pieces. Top the casserole evenly with the cracker crumbs and dot with butter. Bake until the cracker crumbs are golden and the casserole is bubbling, 35 to 45 minutes.

Butter-Poached Shrimp

WITH TOMATOES AND BASIL OVER ANGEL HAIR PASTA

Sometimes the simplest of recipes are the absolute best recipes. You just have to remember that the fewer ingredients called for, the better quality those ingredients have to be. This is definitely the case with this recipe. Your tomatoes must be at the peak of ripeness. Fresh Gulf shrimp are a must and the basil has to be fresh. I came up with this recipe for the first "tomato dinner" Luke and I hosted on our farm—an event that has become an annual tradition. When the tomatoes are in season and we have them coming out of our ears, these dinners are one way we share them with the community. Tomatoes are served for every course. Even the specialty cocktail and the dessert include tomatoes!

SERVES 6 TO 8

Salt

1 pound angel hair pasta

1 pound (4 sticks) salted butter

8 cloves garlic, minced

3 pounds large (21/25) peeled and deveined shrimp

4 cups chopped fresh tomatoes or halved cherry tomatoes

½ cup chopped fresh basil

½ cup grated parmesan cheese

1. Bring a large pot of salted water to a boil and cook the pasta according to package instructions.

2. Meanwhile, melt the butter in a large pot over medium-high heat. Add the garlic and cook until fragrant, 2 to 3 minutes. Add the shrimp, reduce the heat to maintain a low simmer, and poach until the shrimp are pink and cooked all the way through, 5 to 7 minutes.

3. When the pasta is done, drain it thoroughly in a colander in the sink.

4. Add the tomatoes to the shrimp mixture and remove from the heat. Add the cooked pasta and toss well. Garnish with the fresh basil and parmesan. Serve immediately. (This is also a great dish at room temperature.)

Chef Tip The way you determine the size of the shrimp is based on how many are in a pound. For example, 21/25 means there are 21 to 25 shrimp in each pound.

GRANDMOTHER'S
Mocha Cake

Everything my grandmother cooked was sheer perfection. If it wasn't, you sure wouldn't know about it. If she was baking a cake and it split or just didn't turn out right, she would go outside, dig a hole, and bury it so that no one would see it in the garbage can and know she had made a mistake. (These are the kind of people I come from and I couldn't be any prouder!) This mocha cake was one of her specialties. When we would come to visit, it was always on her covered glass cake stand. It was two square layers, only iced in the middle and on the top; the sides were left naked. She would sprinkle chopped pecans over the top of the thick mocha icing. Some families have skeletons buried in their backyards. In our backyards, we just have cakes!

SERVES 10

½ pound (2 sticks) salted butter, plus more for the pans

Pinch of salt

2 cups sugar

4 large eggs

1 (4-ounce) package Baker's German's Sweet Chocolate (there is no substitution), melted and cooled slightly

2½ cups cake flour

1 teaspoon baking soda

1 cup buttermilk

Mocha Icing (page 128)

1 cup finely chopped pecans

1. Preheat the oven to 375°F. Grease two 8-inch square cake pans and line them with parchment paper.

2. In a large bowl, using an electric mixer, cream the butter and salt. With the mixer running, add the sugar 1 tablespoon at a time, until the mixture is well blended. Add the eggs one at a time, making sure each is thoroughly combined before adding the next one. Add the chocolate and mix until blended through.

3. Sift the flour and baking soda together three times. Add the flour mixture and buttermilk to the chocolate mixture in alternate batches, starting and ending with the flour, using a rubber spatula to fold them in. Divide the batter between the prepared pans.

4. Bake until a toothpick inserted in the center comes out clean, about 35 minutes. (Do not overbake.) Let cool completely in the pans.

5. Unmold the cakes from the pans, remove the paper from the bottoms, and set one layer on a serving plate. Spread half the icing over the bottom layer and then set the second layer on top. Spread with the remaining icing, then cover with chopped pecans.

MOCHA ICING

MAKES ABOUT 4½ CUPS

1 teaspoon unsweetened cocoa powder

¼ cup hot coffee

4 tablespoons (½ stick) unsalted butter

1 (1-pound) package powdered sugar (about 4 cups), sifted

1 teaspoon vanilla extract

1. In a small bowl or measuring cup, stir the cocoa powder into the hot coffee until dissolved. In a large bowl using an electric mixer, cream the butter and sugar until light and fluffy. Add the vanilla. Add the coffee mixture a little at a time until the icing reaches a spreadable consistency. Use immediately.

Chocolate Cobbler

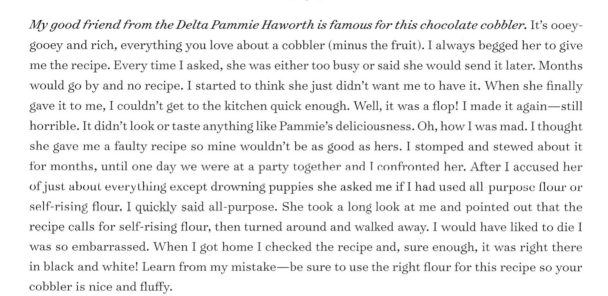

My good friend from the Delta Pammie Haworth is famous for this chocolate cobbler. It's ooey-gooey and rich, everything you love about a cobbler (minus the fruit). I always begged her to give me the recipe. Every time I asked, she was either too busy or said she would send it later. Months would go by and no recipe. I started to think she just didn't want me to have it. When she finally gave it to me, I couldn't get to the kitchen quick enough. Well, it was a flop! I made it again—still horrible. It didn't look or taste anything like Pammie's deliciousness. Oh, how I was mad. I thought she gave me a faulty recipe so mine wouldn't be as good as hers. I stomped and stewed about it for months, until one day we were at a party together and I confronted her. After I accused her of just about everything except drowning puppies she asked me if I had used all-purpose flour or self-rising flour. I quickly said all-purpose. She took a long look at me and pointed out that the recipe calls for self-rising flour, then turned around and walked away. I would have liked to die I was so embarrassed. When I got home I checked the recipe and, sure enough, it was right there in black and white! Learn from my mistake—be sure to use the right flour for this recipe so your cobbler is nice and fluffy.

SERVES 8

½ pound (2 sticks) salted butter

2½ cups sugar

1½ cups self-rising flour

¾ cup milk

1 tablespoon vanilla extract

6 tablespoons unsweetened cocoa powder

¾ cup very hot water

1. Preheat the oven to 350°F.

2. Melt the butter and pour it into a large ovenproof skillet or 9 x 13-inch baking dish. In a large bowl, combine 1½ cups of the sugar, the flour, milk, and vanilla. Mix well and pour over the melted butter in the baking dish.

3. In another bowl, mix together the remaining 1 cup sugar and the cocoa powder. Sift over the batter in the baking dish.

4. Pour the hot water over the top. Bake for 30 to 35 minutes, until the cobbler is set. Serve immediately.

5

BEACH DAYS

Growing up, my parents kept us kids' expectations really low. They would take us to the Mississippi River sandbar and tell us we were at the beach. So you can imagine how excited I was on my first trip to Florida. I remember looking at Daddy and asking him in complete seriousness, "Where is the other side of this water?"

There is hardly a place I love more than the beach, and now I look forward to taking my children to the beach each summer. Once I get there I do not want to do a single thing . . . except, of course, drink too much, eat too much, and sit in the sun way too much. In order for all these too-muches to happen according to plan, some serious prep work must be undertaken before the car is packed and we head south. I do a lot of cooking before any beach trip. That way, if I want to stay on the beach until the sun goes down, drinking the last can of beer in the cooler, nothing will stop me.

Cornbread Salad

————◇◇◇————

Whenever I make cornbread muffins, I double the recipe. Hardly anything freezes as well as cornbread does. Once the cornbread has cooled, I put it in a Ziploc bag and into the freezer it goes. Then I can pull out a few cornbread muffins anytime to go with dinner. This cornbread salad is super simple, especially if you already have the cornbread in the freezer.

SERVES 10

1 (1-ounce) package ranch dressing mix

1½ cups sour cream

1½ cups mayonnaise

1 recipe cornbread (page 103), cooled and crumbled

10 slices bacon, cooked and chopped (reserve the grease for another use)

8 ounces cheddar cheese, shredded by hand using a box grater (2 cups)

3 fresh medium tomatoes, chopped

2 (15-ounce) cans whole kernel corn, drained

1 cup chopped red bell pepper (about 1 pepper)

1 cup chopped green onions (white and green parts)

½ head iceberg lettuce, thinly sliced

1. In a medium bowl, whisk together the ranch dressing mix, sour cream, and mayonnaise. Set aside.

2. Place half of the cornbread crumbles on the bottom of a glass serving dish followed by half each of the bacon, cheese, tomatoes, corn, bell pepper, green onions, and lettuce. Drizzle with half of the ranch dressing mixture.

3. Repeat these layers, reserving a little bit of everything for the top. For the last layer, toss the reserved ingredients together and scatter on top, then drizzle with more dressing. Cover and refrigerate for at least 2 hours before serving.

Dessert No. 4

For a while after Luke and I got married, I used to make this recipe every chance I got. It is one of those recipes that is so easy—you make it ahead of time and freeze it—but always gets rave reviews. Eventually a friend asked if I knew any other recipes besides "the ice cream sandwich dessert." At that point, I put the recipe on the shelf and forgot about it until my good friend Kate Green reminded me about it recently. Her mom called it Dessert No. 4. This recipe calls for blonde ice cream sandwiches, but you can always substitute the chocolate ones. If you prefer not to use alcohol there is nothing wrong with subbing chocolate or caramel sauce.

SERVES 10

Cooking spray

½ cup silvered almonds

12 ice cream sandwiches with vanilla crackers

¾ cup amaretto

1 (12-ounce) container Cool Whip

1 (8-ounce) package toffee bits

1. Preheat the oven to 300°F. Grease a 9 x 13-inch baking dish with cooking spray.

2. Spread the almonds on a baking sheet and bake until lightly toasted, about 5 minutes. (Keep an eye on them, they will burn quickly.) Set aside.

3. Line the baking dish with the ice cream sandwiches in a single layer. Drizzle half the amaretto over the sandwiches. Mix the remaining amaretto into the Cool Whip.

4. Sprinkle half of the toffee bits over the sandwiches. Spread with the Cool Whip mixture. Sprinkle the rest of the toffee bits and the almonds on top. Cover and freeze until you're ready to serve, at least 3 hours and up to 4 months.

HUMBLE
Chicken Salad

There are so many chicken salad recipes in the world, it is hard to keep count—and I honestly think I have tried just about all of them. In addition, there are almost as many opinions about chicken salad. People have very strong opinions about adding fruit or nuts or sour cream. Even the texture of the chicken can be debated for hours. My recipe is simple and not too fancy, but in my humble opinion, it is one damn fine chicken salad. Everyone who eats it loves it. The most important part of this recipe is cooking the chicken. The recipe is so simple that the chicken has to be perfect. While lots of other recipes call for chicken chunks, notice I tell you to shred the chicken. I can't even say the word chunk and certainly won't eat one so for this recipe, so prepare to shred the chicken.

SERVES 6 TO 8

8 bone-in, skin-on chicken breasts

5 tablespoons Cavender's Greek seasoning

2 stalks celery, finely chopped

2 cups mayonnaise, plus more if needed

1. Place the chicken breasts in a large pot and cover with cold water. Sprinkle 4 tablespoons of Greek seasoning on the water. Stir together the water, chicken, and seasoning. Bring to a boil over high heat and then reduce to a simmer. Simmer the chicken for 45 minutes, until no longer pink inside. Turn off the heat and let the chicken sit in the water for another 15 minutes.

2. Remove the chicken, let cool to room temperature, and reserve 2 tablespoons of the chicken cooking water.

3. When cool enough to handle, separate the chicken from the skin and bones. Shred the chicken meat into a large bowl. Discard the skin and bones.

4. Add the celery, mayonnaise, the reserved cooking water, and the remaining tablespoon Greek seasoning to the chicken. Stir gently to mix all the ingredients. Taste and adjust the seasoning, adding more mayonnaise if you prefer. Serve immediately, or refrigerate, covered, for up to 4 days.

Seaside Shrimp

When I am at the beach, the last thing I want to do is stay in the kitchen all day while my entire family plays on the sand. That is why I do so much prep ahead of time and then take everything down with me. The one problem with that approach is that I want to eat shrimp fresh from the beach. There is nothing better than the taste of fresh Gulf shrimp. This recipe is so great because I can make the marinade at home and store it in a big mason jar. Once I get to the shore, all I have to do is boil the shrimp, add the marinade and a few veggies, and I am back on the beach in no time.

SERVES 8

1 tablespoon concentrated liquid crab boil

2 pounds peeled and deveined large (21/25) shrimp

2 pounds fresh okra, stemmed and sliced in half lengthwise

1 red bell pepper, thinly sliced

1 orange bell pepper, thinly sliced

1 cup thinly sliced sweet onion (1 onion)

1 cup cherry tomatoes, cut in half

¼ cup white balsamic vinegar

2 teaspoons kosher salt

½ teaspoon pepper

2 large lemons, 1 juiced, 1 sliced into rounds, seeds removed

2 bay leaves

¼ teaspoon red pepper flakes

¾ cup olive oil

½ cup thinly sliced fresh basil

1. In a large stockpot, bring 4 quarts water and the liquid crab boil to a full boil. Add the shrimp and boil for about 3 minutes, until pink and cooked through. Drain the shrimp in a colander in the sink and run cold water over them to stop the cooking process. Drain well.

2. Combine the shrimp, okra, bell peppers, onion, and tomatoes in a pretty glass serving bowl.

3. Whisk the vinegar, salt, pepper, lemon juice, bay leaves, and red pepper flakes in a small bowl. Slowly drizzle in the oil, whisking constantly, until the dressing is emulsified. Set aside.

4. Add the sliced lemon to the shrimp mixture. Pour over the dressing and stir to combine. Cover and refrigerate for at least 8 hours, stirring occasionally.

5. Remove the bay leaves and add the basil just before serving.

CORN AND RED ONION
Guacamole

I got my first catering job when I was in high school, at a company called Another Roadside Attraction, owned by a friend of my mother's. The owner, Karen, had booked a huge wedding for a lovely couple in Memphis. They decided to have food stations representing each place they had ever lived. So there was a St. Louis station, one for Italy, France, New Orleans; the list went on and on. This was at least twenty-six years ago, well before anyone was doing creative things with wedding food. Karen needed lots of help feeding the hundreds of guests, so Mom volunteered me to go and work. It was the most amazing night and I was totally hooked. Now, all these years later, I am still hooked! The couple was going to honeymoon in Mexico, so of course they had to have a taco and tequila station; this guacamole was one of the recipes they served.

SERVES 4

1 ear fresh corn, in the husk

4 ripe avocados

½ red onion, finely chopped

½ jalapeño, finely chopped

1 bunch cilantro, chopped

2 to 4 teaspoons fresh lime juice

Salt and pepper

Chef Tip Never buy bags of avocados. You need to be able to squeeze each one of them to make sure they are good. You just want it to give a little bit when you squeeze it. If it has sunken-in places, it is too ripe. If it doesn't give at all, then it is too firm for guacamole. If you are trying to ripen avocados, store them in a paper bag. If you want to slow down the ripening process, put them in the refrigerator.

1. Preheat the oven to 350°F. Cut off the silk at the end of the corn. Place the corn on a baking sheet and roast for about 30 minutes, until warm to the touch and slightly brown. Let cool until you can handle the corn. Remove the husk and silk from the corn. Cut the kernels off of the cob.

2. Pit the avocados and scoop the flesh into a bowl; discard the skins. Mash the avocados until creamy, leaving a few lumps for texture. Add the corn, onion, jalapeño, cilantro, and lime juice to taste. Mix well and season with salt and pepper to taste. Serve immediately.

SMOKED

SMOKED
Tuna Dip

As soon as we get to the beach, I get a very serious craving for this dip. I really don't even think about it any other time. It is almost like a Pavlovian response! I hear the waves, see the ocean, and I taste tuna dip. Now, you can certainly substitute any fish for the tuna. A white, flaky fish will do the trick every time. Being from the Delta I have made it using catfish as well. I really love the balance of seasoning in this recipe but feel free to play with it and make it your own. I like to serve this dip with saltine crackers but I have, on occasion, been known to serve it with pork skins as well.

SERVES 4

2 tablespoons mayonnaise

¼ cup sour cream

4 ounces (half an 8-ounce package) cream cheese, room temperature

2 cups flaked cooked fresh tuna

2 green onions (white and green parts), finely chopped

2 teaspoons fresh lemon juice

5 drops hot sauce

4 drops Worcestershire sauce

3 drops liquid smoke

½ teaspoon Creole seasoning (preferably Tony Chachere's)

1. Place the mayonnaise, sour cream, and cream cheese in a food processor and blend until smooth. Add the fish, green onions, lemon juice, hot sauce, Worcestershire, liquid smoke, and Creole seasoning. Blend until the dip has a spreadable consistency. Serve immediately, or refrigerate, covered, up to 4 days.

Shrimp, Corn, Potato, and Sausage Boil

———⬦⟨∞⟩⬦———

If I ask my husband to go to the grocery store and then cook supper, you would think I had asked him to climb a mountain. If I ask this same man to go to the fish market and get the big pot and burner out of the storeroom for a shrimp boil, well, he just can't move fast enough! There must be something about being able to cook outside, using fire, with a beer in his hand, that makes a shrimp boil so appealing. In Mississippi, we use crawfish; when we head to the beach, we bring the big pot and burner and use shrimp instead. We always reserve one night for a shrimp boil. It's a one-pot supper that is super easy to prepare with not much to clean up. That's a beach bonus! We always cook more shrimp than we need. That way there are leftovers for shrimp salad, shrimp dip (see page 149), or just for lunch the next day. Serve the shrimp boil with cocktail sauce, remoulade, or garlic mayo.

SERVES 20

4 tablespoons concentrated liquid crab boil (such as Zatarain's)

2 pounds smoked sausage, cut into 1-inch pieces

12 new potatoes

4 medium onions, peeled and quartered

4 heads garlic, sliced in half crosswise

6 lemons, halved crosswise

6 pounds large (21/25 count) shrimp, with shells and heads on

3 or 4 ears fresh corn, husked, silk removed, cut into 3-inch pieces

4 cups drained artichoke hearts (from four 14-ounce cans)

1. Mix 10 quarts water and the crab boil in a very large stockpot. Bring to a boil over high heat. Add the sausage, potatoes, onions, and garlic and return to a boil. Cover and let boil for 15 minutes.

2. Squeeze the lemons into the water and then throw the rinds into the pot. Add the shrimp, corn, and artichokes and bring back to a boil. Continue boiling for 6 minutes.

3. Drain off the water very well and serve.

LEFTOVER
Shrimp Boil Dip

—◦⟨⟩◦—

You'll need some extra corn to make this dip, which is a great way to transform leftovers into the star of the show. Serve with crackers or tortilla chips.

SERVES 6

2 cups leftover shrimp, or 1 pound peeled cooked shrimp, cut into ½-inch pieces

4 ears corn, kernels cut from the cobs

1 cup leftover smoked sausage, cut into ½-inch pieces

1 cup mayonnaise

1 medium red onion, chopped (¾ cup)

½ cup chopped fresh cilantro

2 tablespoons fresh lime juice

1 teaspoon ground cumin

1 teaspoon Creole seasoning (preferably Tony Chachere's)

4 dashes hot sauce

1. Mix together all the ingredients in a large bowl. Serve immediately or store in an airtight container for up to 3 days.

PEACH AND BLUEBERRY
Cobbler

On the way to Florida from Oxford, we pass through a most peculiar town. It has a water tower that quite literally moons drivers on the interstate. It looks like a giant blushing heinie. Yep! It is the peach-shaped water tower of Chilton County, Alabama. Chilton County is famous for two things that I know of: garbage bag peaches and the peach-butt water tower. "Garbage bag peaches?" you ask? Why yes, these are the kind of plump, ripe peaches you literally have to eat over a garbage can because they drip so much juice. We always stop on our way to the beach in the summertime to buy a case of peaches for the week.

This cobbler is super easy to throw together so you can get back to beach business: drinking, eating, and sunning.

SERVES 8

2 cups peeled, sliced peaches (about 4 peaches)

2 cups fresh blueberries

2 cups sugar

8 tablespoons (1 stick) salted butter

1½ cups self-rising flour

1½ cups milk

1 teaspoon ground cinnamon (optional)

Whipped cream or vanilla ice cream, for serving

1. Preheat the oven to 350°F.

2. Combine the peaches, blueberries, 1 cup of the sugar, and ½ cup water in a saucepan and mix well. Bring to a boil, then simmer for about 10 minutes. Remove from the heat.

3. Put the butter in a large ovenproof skillet or 3-quart baking dish and place in the oven to melt.

4. Mix the remaining 1 cup sugar, the flour, and milk slowly to prevent clumping. Pour the mixture over the melted butter. Do not stir. Spoon the fruit on top, gently pouring in the syrup. Sprinkle the top with cinnamon (if using). Bake for 30 to 45 minutes, until golden-brown. (The batter will rise to the top during baking.)

5. To serve, scoop onto plates. Serve with your choice of whipped cream or vanilla ice cream.

Fish Tacos
WITH LIME CREMA

—◇◇◇—

I don't know what it is about a fish taco, but if there is one on a menu you can bet your life on me ordering it. Even if I was in Kansas, a state that couldn't be any more landlocked, I'd have the fish tacos. If I see "fish taco," I am sold! When serving them at home or for a party, it's so fun to put out tons of toppings so that guests or family can help themselves.

SERVES 8

4 cups yellow cornmeal

4 teaspoons Cajun seasoning

4 teaspoons seasoned salt

2 teaspoons Cavender's Greek seasoning

6 (6-ounce) flounder or grouper fillets (or any other mild white fish)

Vegetable oil, for frying

2 cups sour cream

½ cup chopped fresh cilantro

Juice of 1 lime

1 teaspoon ground cumin

Salt and pepper

8 to 12 flour or corn tortillas

Additional toppings, such as shredded cabbage, lime wedges, sliced jalapeños, chopped fresh tomatoes, and sliced avocado

1. Combine the cornmeal, Cajun seasoning, seasoned salt, and Greek seasoning in a shallow bowl. Mix well. Dredge the fish in the cornmeal mixture and shake off any excess. Set aside on a platter while the oil heats.

2. Pour oil into a Dutch oven or cast-iron pot to the depth of 2 inches. Heat the oil to 350°F. Fry the fish in batches, until the fillets float to the top of the oil and are golden brown, 3 to 5 minutes. Drain the fillets on paper towels.

Chef Tip When deep-frying anything, the best way to know if it is done is if it floats to the top of the oil. This is true for everything from oysters to chicken to hushpuppies.

3. While the fish is frying, in a medium bowl, mix the sour cream, cilantro, lime juice, and cumin. Mix well and season with salt and pepper to taste.

4. Chop the fillets into bite-size pieces. Place the fish in the tortillas and top with the lime crema. Serve with any desired toppings.

Mom Tip When I would make up lots of fish tacos for a crowd, I would get so frustrated because I wanted the soft tacos to stand up like a hard-shell taco for a pretty presentation. A friend who is a genius suggested I use a wooden plate-drying rack, the kind you find at the dollar store! It was perfect. Now I make a taco, nestle it between the wooden spindles, and move onto the next one.

6

GAME DAYS

We may not win every game, but we will damn sure win every party!

I have never been very athletic. I always was the last one picked for dodgeball. And I didn't play any sports in high school. Honestly, I couldn't have cared less. It wasn't until we moved to Oxford, home of the Ole Miss Rebels, that I discovered my competitive side. Ole Miss is known for the most extravagant tailgates in the South. On game days, their campus tailgating field, known as The Grove, is covered in a sea of tents as far as the eye can see. These aren't just any tents. They are adorned with crisp linens, crystal chandeliers, and silver candelabra. Now, this pregame is the kind of thing I can get behind. I figured out that my sport is tailgating. When I leave The Grove to go into the stadium to watch the game, rest assured, I have already won the competition.

PB & J Wings

I have never met anyone as regimented as my friend Jed. He is a marathon runner, doesn't drink to excess, and eats extremely healthy—except for Friday nights, when he eats a large steak and homemade mac-n-cheese. Jed rarely splurges, but when he does, stand back because it's about to get serious! Once he got on a wing kick for a while and for weeks he tried all kinds of recipes. Fried ones, Asian sticky ones, grilled ones, and a version made with PB & J. I know what you are thinking: PB & J wings? Don't roll your eyes just yet and don't judge this recipe. There is something about the sweetness of the jelly and the earthiness of the peanut butter with the spice of the sriracha that is just amazing.

SERVES 6

¼ cup grape jelly

3 tablespoons bourbon

2 tablespoons smooth peanut butter

2 tablespoons Worcestershire sauce

2 tablespoons light brown sugar

1 tablespoon tomato-based chili sauce (preferably Heinz)

2 teaspoons paprika

1 teaspoon sriracha

2 pounds chicken wings

2 tablespoons chopped peanuts, for garnish

Fresh cilantro, for garnish

1. In a small bowl, mix the jelly, bourbon, peanut butter, Worcestershire, brown sugar, chili sauce, paprika, and sriracha.

2. Pour half of the sauce into a Ziploc bag; set aside the rest to baste the wings during cooking. Add the chicken wings to the sauce in the bag, zip up the bag, and marinate in the refrigerator for at least 2 hours (overnight is even better).

3. Heat the grill to medium heat. Remove the wings from the marinade and shake off any excess marinade. (This will help avoid flare-ups.)

4. Grill, turning often so the wings don't burn before they are cooked all the way through, about 35 minutes total. Once the wings are a few minutes from being done, baste with the remaining sauce. Let the sauce caramelize and the wings finish cooking; an instant-read thermometer inserted into the meaty part, not touching bone, should read 165°F. Remove from the grill and garnish with the chopped peanuts and cilantro.

BISCUIT BAR
OR
NACHO BAR

Many game days start very early. This means the drinking starts just as early. With such a long day ahead of you, you must pace yourself and eat to ensure you don't end up tipsy before noon. A biscuit bar in the morning is the perfect way to make sure everyone gets to the game in perfect form. Once the biscuits are made, it is really just a matter of purchasing and assembling. Serve a buffet of buttermilk biscuits, spiral-sliced ham, chicken tenders, bacon, sliced tomatoes, sausage patties, preserves, jams, jellies, honey, strawberry butter . . . the list goes on and on.

Now, an evening game can be just as tricky. Many times these games go late into the night and you need to fortify yourself. If you're watching the game at home, nachos are always a crowd-pleaser. I have what I call purchase-and-put-out nachos: You can buy most of your toppings at the store. Grab some super cute wooden and tin serving pieces and go to town. Chips, salsa, guacamole, sour cream, pulled rotisserie chicken, shredded cheese, black olives, jalapeño peppers, cilantro.

JAMBALAYA
Fried Chicken Pasta

On big game weekends, everyone welcomes company from out of town with open arms. The only problem is our friends come back to Oxford and tend to act just like they did in college. They want to go visit all the old bars and drink entirely too much. This trip down memory lane wouldn't be complete without a trip to the Chevron gas station for their famous chicken on a stick. As soon as the bars let out, everyone walks to "Chicken on a Stick" and lines up. What in the world could be so great that young and old will stand in a line at 1:00 a.m.? It is fried chicken on a stick and it's heavenly. Once you make it to the counter you are so excited and hungry you can't help but overorder. Pizza rolls, potato logs, and six chicken-on-a-sticks. Inevitably there are lots of leftovers the next morning. This is when jambalaya fried chicken pasta was born. After one such night I was making pasta jambalaya for tailgating at The Grove. Instead of putting in my normal rotisserie chicken, I added leftover fried chicken from the Chevron. My goodness, it was sheer magic. If you aren't lucky enough to live in Oxford, you can use any fried chicken tenders. This recipe has a lot of steps and ingredients, but it is well worth the effort.

SERVES 6

1 pound penne pasta

2 tablespoons olive oil

1 pound peeled and deveined large (21/25) shrimp

2 tablespoons plus 1 teaspoon Cajun seasoning

3 pounds andouille sausage, cut into ½-inch pieces

½ cup chopped yellow onion (about ½ onion)

½ cup chopped green bell pepper (about ½ pepper)

1 tablespoon minced garlic

½ cup chicken broth

1 (14.5-ounce) can diced tomatoes, with their juices

1 tablespoon fresh thyme leaves

½ cup heavy cream

6 cups chopped fried chicken pieces (about 6 fried chicken tenders)

2 tablespoons chopped fresh basil

½ cup grated parmesan cheese

1. Cook the pasta in boiling salted water (use at least 1 teaspoon salt in the water) until al dente, according to the package instructions. Reserve 1 cup of the pasta water; drain the pasta.

2. Meanwhile, in a large skillet over medium heat, heat 1 tablespoon of the olive oil, swirling the pan to coat evenly.

3. Mix the shrimp with 2 tablespoons of the Cajun seasoning. Add the shrimp to the hot oil and cook for 1 minute per side, turning once, until opaque and slightly firm. Remove the shrimp from the pan and set aside.

4. Add the remaining tablespoon olive oil to the pan, then add the sausage, onion, and bell pepper. Sauté until the sausage is caramelized and the onion is translucent. Add the garlic and sauté for a few seconds, then add the chicken broth. Scrape the bottom of the pan to remove any tiny brown bits that have formed. Add the tomatoes, thyme, and the remaining 1 teaspoon Cajun seasoning and cook for 2 minutes.

5. Stir in the heavy cream. Then add the shrimp, pasta, and reserved pasta water. Continue to cook until the sauce has thickened a bit, about 15 minutes.

6. Remove from the heat and add the fried chicken pieces, basil, and parmesan. Toss to combine, then serve hot.

SIMPLE

SIMPLE
Potato Salad

Poor, poor potato salad. So often it gets overlooked on a buffet, only put on a plate if there is extra room. It can be bland or boring—certainly not the star of the show. But if you take some time with it and really make sure you get the seasoning correct, you won't believe the oohs and aahs this poor-no-more potato salad will get. Try to select the smallest potatoes you can find. Make sure they are very firm to the touch and that the skin is as smooth as a baby's bottom. You also don't want to select a potato where the eyes have started sprouting. That potato is ready to be planted, not eaten!

SERVES 12

24 small new potatoes (about 3 pounds), skin on, well scrubbed

½ cup mayonnaise

½ cup sour cream

2 tablespoons finely chopped fresh dill

2 tablespoons finely chopped fresh parsley

2 teaspoons grated lemon zest

1 tablespoon fresh lemon juice

1½ teaspoons Cajun seasoning or seasoned salt

2 stalks celery, diced

¼ cup finely chopped green onions (white and green parts)

Salt and pepper

1. Cover the potatoes with cold water in a large pot. Bring the water to a boil and cook until a knife can be inserted into the potatoes easily, 10 to 12 minutes; don't boil so long that the potatoes split. (If you overcook them, you will end up with mashed potatoes, not potato salad.)

2. Drain the potatoes and let cool enough for you to handle them. Cut each potato into bite-size pieces and place in a large bowl.

3. In a small bowl, combine the mayo, sour cream, dill, parsley, lemon zest, lemon juice, and Cajun seasoning.

4. Add the celery, green onions, and mayonnaise mixture to the potatoes. Season with salt and pepper to taste. Mix gently but well. Cover and refrigerate for at least 3 hours before serving. (This can be made a couple of days in advance; it only gets better as it sits. If you store the potato salad for a few days you might need to add a little more mayonnaise and salt and pepper before serving. As the potatoes sit overnight they will absorb some of the dressing and can become a little dry.)

Grillades and Grits

This recipe might not win any beauty pageants but I daresay it is the best recipe out of this whole book. Not everyone is a beauty queen! You may not want to take it with you to your tailgate, but it is perfect for having friends over to watch the game. Grillades—a kind of beef or veal stew—originated in New Orleans and is traditionally served at Mardi Gras and debutante brunches. It is most people's opinion that the New Orleans Country Club has the best recipe, and its grillades are the ones that all others must be measured against. I once made these for a brunch attended by a lovely gentleman who was a fourth-generation New Orleanian. He knew grillades and grits like the back of his hand. I watched from across the room and held my breath as he put the grillades and grits into his mouth. When he smiled, I exhaled. A few minutes later he stopped me and whispered in my ear, "Your grillades are better than the country club's." He didn't say which country club so I will forever assume he meant the New Orleans Country Club.

SERVES 10

4 pounds boneless beef or veal top round steaks

½ cup bacon grease or vegetable oil

½ cup all-purpose flour

2 cups chopped green onions (white and green parts)

1½ cups chopped green bell peppers

1 cup chopped onion (about 1 onion)

¾ cup chopped celery (3 to 4 stalks)

2 cloves garlic, minced

2 cups chopped fresh tomatoes, or 1 (15-ounce) can

¾ teaspoon dried thyme

½ teaspoon dried tarragon (optional)

1 cup red wine

2 tablespoons Worcestershire sauce

1 tablespoon salt

½ teaspoon pepper

2 bay leaves

½ teaspoon Tabasco sauce

3 tablespoons chopped fresh parsley

Baked Grits (recipe follows), for serving

1. Remove any fat from the meat and cut the meat into 4-inch pieces. Pound each piece to ¼ inch thick.

2. In a Dutch oven over medium-high heat, working in batches if necessary, brown the meat well in ¼ cup of the bacon grease. As the meat browns, remove to a warm plate.

3. When all the meat is browned, add the remaining ¼ cup bacon grease and the flour to the pot. Stirring constantly, cook to make a dark brown roux, about 15 minutes. (Do not let it burn.)

4. Add the green onions, bell peppers, onion, celery, and garlic to the roux and sauté until the vegetables are limp, about 5 minutes, making sure you constantly stir and scrape the bottom of the pan.

5. Add the tomatoes, thyme, and tarragon (if using), and cook for about 3 minutes.

6. Add 1 cup water and the wine. Stir well for several minutes. Return the meat and any juices to the pot and add the Worcestershire, salt, pepper, bay leaves, and Tabasco.

7. Lower the heat to maintain a simmer. If using veal, simmer covered, stirring occasionally, for approximately 1 hour. If using beef, simmer covered for approximately 2 hours. The grillades should be very tender.

8. Remove the bay leaves and stir in the parsley, then let cool. Let the grillades sit for several hours or overnight in the refrigerator for the flavors to develop. When ready to serve, reheat in the pot, adding water if you need more liquid. Serve over the grits.

BAKED GRITS

SERVES 10

1 tablespoon salt

2 cups grits

6 ounces cheddar cheese, grated (about 1½ cups)

3 cloves garlic, minced or pressed

8 tablespoons (1 stick) salted butter, plus more for the baking dish

3 eggs, slightly beaten

2 cups milk

2 cups grated parmesan cheese

1. Preheat the oven to 325°F and thoroughly grease a 9 x 13-inch baking dish. Combine 2 quarts water and the salt in a large pot and bring to a boil.

2. Add the grits and cook, stirring often, until tender but still pourable, about 12 minutes. Remove from the heat. Add the cheese, garlic, and butter and stir until the cheese and butter are melted. Let cool to room temperature.

3. Stir the eggs and milk into the grits. Pour the mixture into the prepared baking dish. Bake for 50 to 60 minutes, until the center is set and top is golden. Remove from the oven and sprinkle with the parmesan. Return to the oven and bake until the cheese is melted, about 10 minutes more. Serve immediately.

4. To make the grits ahead of time, prepare all the way through spreading the grits in the baking dish in step 3. Cover and refrigerate for up to 4 days. When you're ready to bake, pull it out of the fridge, uncover, and bake as directed.

1-2-3
Chess Squares

There is nothing better than a pick-up sweet on the menu at a tailgate. What, might you ask, is a "pick-up sweet"? A small dessert you can pick up with one hand and eat without putting your drink down. Any brownie, lemon square, or chess square will do. I love having a nice assortment—that way people can have a little bite of lemon, chocolate, and vanilla. This recipe is as easy as 1-2-3 because it uses a boxed cake mix. Normally I just buy a basic butter cake mix, but when I'm feeling a little on the wild side, I have been known to use a devil's food cake or strawberry cake mix instead.

If you want a little lemon flavor, you can always add the juice and grated zest of 1 lemon to the cream cheese mixture and omit the vanilla.

SERVES 12

1 box yellow cake mix, such as Duncan Hines

½ pound (2 sticks) butter, melted

3 large eggs

1 cup pecans, chopped (optional)

2 (8-ounce) packages cream cheese, room temperature

1 (1-pound) package powdered sugar (4 cups)

Chef Tip Let me make your life easier. For these chess squares, brownies, or any other dessert baked in a pan that you need to cut into squares, line the pan with foil first. Make sure the foil overhangs the sides of the pan. This makes it a breeze to remove the dessert from the pan.

1. Preheat the oven to 350°F. Line a 9 x 13-inch pan with foil or parchment paper, making sure the foil or paper hangs over the edges of the pan.

2. In a large bowl, mix together the cake mix, butter, and 1 egg. Stir in the pecans (if using.) Press the mixture into the bottom of the prepared pan.

3. In the bowl of a stand mixer fitted with a paddle attachment, beat the cream cheese with the powdered sugar until well combined and fluffy. Add the remaining 2 eggs one at a time, making sure the first is thoroughly combined before adding the next one.

4. Pour the cream cheese mixture over the crust. Bake for about 45 minutes, until the center is set. Let cool completely in the pan. Once cooled, use the foil to lift the dessert out of the pan. Cut into squares and serve. Store in an airtight container in the fridge for up to 6 days.

Nuts and Bolts

There are some recipes I almost feel guilty sharing. If I know on the front end that a recipe is highly addictive, death to a diet, and super simple to make, I almost feel like a drug dealer. This is one of those. On the other hand, I would hate for everyone to not be able to enjoy this most perfect game day snack. It's simple to make, can be made ahead, and freezes beautifully. What more could you ask for? So here it goes, but make it at your own risk and know you have been warned.

SERVES 10

3 cups Corn Chex cereal

3 cups Wheat Chex cereal

1 cup pretzel sticks

1 cup Cheez-Its

1 cup dry-roasted peanuts

2 tablespoons salted butter

⅓ cup buffalo wing sauce (not hot sauce)

1 (1-ounce) packet ranch dressing mix

1. Line a rimmed baking sheet with foil.

2. In a large microwave-safe bowl, combine the Chex cereals, pretzels, Cheez-Its, and peanuts.

3. In a small pot over medium heat, melt the butter. Whisk in the buffalo sauce and ranch dressing mix. Pour half of the sauce over the Chex mixture and stir very well. Then pour the rest of the sauce over the Chex mixture and mix very well.

4. Microwave the Chex mixture for 2 minutes on high. Remove and stir; repeat this process two more times (6 minutes total). Remove from the microwave and spread the mixture onto the prepared baking sheet. Allow to cool for 30 to 45 minutes before serving. Store in an airtight container at room temperature for up to 6 weeks. It can be frozen for up to 6 months.

Fireside Dip

A.K.A. HOT TAMALE DIP

Cocktail hour was always a big deal at my grandmother's house. She always put out a beautiful display of cheeses and crackers or at the very least a silver bowl of nuts. I wasn't a big fan of the Gorgonzola, Brie, or Triscuits when I was young, and nobody was offering me a scotch, so cocktail hour was pretty boring. Except for the times grandmother would make this dip and break out the Fritos. Oh, the glory days! Every time I make this, I am transported back to my grandmother's den. How amazing that one dip can bring so much happiness.

SERVES 6

2 green onions (white and green parts), finely chopped

3 tablespoons salted butter

1 (10-ounce) can Ro*Tel tomatoes

1 (19-ounce) can plain chili, no beans (such as Hormel)

2 (15-ounce) cans Hormel hot beef tamales, coarsely chopped

1 tablespoon Worcestershire sauce

1 teaspoon garlic powder

1 pound sharp cheddar cheese, grated (about 4 cups)

Fritos, for serving

1. In a medium, heavy-bottomed pot over medium heat, sauté the green onions in the butter until fragrant and slightly tender, about 3 minutes.

2. Add the tomatoes and their juices and the chili. Mix very well. Add the tamales, Worcestershire, and garlic powder. Stir well, breaking up the tamales, and cook for 5 minutes, until everything is well mixed. Add the cheese and stir until melted. Serve hot with the Fritos for dipping.

Chef Tip For a little twist, serve this dip with snack bags of Fritos, and offer sour cream, shredded cheddar cheese, chopped onions, and chopped tomatoes. Have guests open the bags and spoon the dip into the bag. After the guests top their bags with the toppings, they can eat right out of the bags with a fork. This is so much fun for kids, not to mention the adults who love to eat like kids.

CHILI-RUBBED

Pork Shoulder Sliders

WITH CANDIED JALAPEÑOS

I don't think I have met a barbecue sandwich that I didn't like. If I am traveling from state to state, I will search out barbecue joints so I can get my fix. Doesn't matter to me if you slather it in a vinegar-based sauce, a mustard-based one, or a sweet-and-hot sauce. I cannot get enough. I have watched grown men get downright mean when discussing what state has the best barbecue: Texas, Tennessee, Arkansas, or Mississippi. I don't know what all the fighting is about. As far as I am concerned, it's all good. These sliders are a perfect way to enjoy BBQ on a game day. Rarely are there seats for everyone to sit down at a tailgate, so you need food that you can easily eat standing up.

Once you top them with candied jalapeños, the deal is sealed. Game over: This barbecue is a winner.

MAKES 24 SLIDERS

24 Hawaiian slider buns, split

Chili-Rubbed Pork Shoulder (page 51)

2 cups of your favorite barbecue sauce

Candied Jalapeños (recipe follows)

1. Remove the tops of the buns. Place the pork on the bun bottoms and top with barbecue sauce and candied jalapeños. Place the top bun back on the sandwich and serve.

CANDIED JALAPEÑOS

MAKES 1½ TO 2 CUPS

1 (12-ounce) jar sliced pickled jalapeños, drained

1 cup sugar

Grated zest of 1 lime

1. Put the jalapeños in a medium bowl. Add the sugar and zest and stir well. Let sit for an hour.

2. Pack into an airtight container or mason jar. Let sit in the fridge for 1 week to let the sugar permeate the jalapeños. After the week is over, enjoy. The jalapeños will keep in the refrigerator for another 2 weeks.

Caramel Brownies

——◇◇◇◇——

When I first started writing cookbooks, I quickly realized that people were going to see how many shortcuts I take. They would know how simple some of my recipes are. So many of my friends would now know that I wasn't slaving over a hot stove, sweating and cussing, to create these culinary treats. Then I remembered the bottom line: I want people to go into the kitchen and cook. I think that it is so important. So if revealing my tricks gets you cooking, then fine. My secret recipes are coming out of the closet. This is one of those secret recipes—it tastes so good but is so easy to make since it uses boxed cake mix and store-bought caramels.

SERVES 12 TO 15

Cooking spray

1 (15.25-ounce) box German chocolate cake mix (I use Betty Crocker)

⅔ cup (about 11 tablespoons) unsalted butter, melted

⅔ cup evaporated milk

1 (11-ounce) bag caramels (such as Kraft)

1½ cups semisweet chocolate chips

Powdered sugar, for dusting (optional)

1. Preheat the oven to 350°F. Grease a 9 x 13-inch baking dish with cooking spray.

2. In a large bowl, mix the cake mix, butter, and ⅓ cup of the evaporated milk. Pour half of the batter into the prepared pan and spread it out; it will be thin. Place the remaining batter in the fridge to chill.

3. Bake the bottom brownie layer for 8 minutes.

4. Meanwhile, unwrap the caramels into a microwave-safe bowl and add the remaining ⅓ cup evaporated milk. Microwave on high in 30-second intervals until the caramels are melted and the mixture is smooth.

5. Remove the brownies from the oven; sprinkle evenly with the chocolate chips and pour the caramel over the chocolate.

6. Remove the chilled batter from the fridge. Scoop 2 tablespoons into the palm of your hand and flatten into a thin layer. Place the pieces over the caramel layer until it is completely covered. Return the brownies to the oven and bake for about 15 minutes more.

7. Allow to cool completely before dusting with powdered sugar (if you'd like) and cutting into squares. (Unless you just cannot wait; then scoop into a bowl and top with ice cream.)

With the right
lunch box fixings
even lunch
period can be a
celebration

7

SCHOOL DAYS

I don't have much sense, but the little bit of sense I do have is really good.

I wasn't the brightest bulb in the box when it came to school. I now know that I had a full-blown case of attention deficit disorder. Not just a touch. Not a tad. A certifiable, card-carrying affliction. I would sit in class and my mind would be 1,000 miles away, usually dreaming about lunch. I loved lunch. Our lunch ladies were just fantastic. The two ladies happened to be sisters. Ask anyone who went to my school and they can recite the lunch schedule. Hamburger Mondays. Spaghetti Wednesdays . . . No matter how tough or frustrating the day was, I always had lunch to look forward to. The lunchroom was my happy place.

When my girls started school, I decided that their lunches should be special as well. I remembered how hard school was so I wanted them to have a bright spot in their busy days. These are some of the recipes I have relied on that go to show that with the right lunch box fixings even lunch period can be a celebration.

No Beans or Greens Chili

One of the first times we took our daughter Lucia out to a nice restaurant, when she was just two, I was super nervous. Our other daughters, Stott and Mary Paxton, had been out a number of times and were old pros. I had checked the menu before we left. I knew they had pasta. Buttered noodles would be Lucia's dining pleasure that evening. An hour into the meal, I had started to relax. The girls were being little angels. The waiter brought us our entrées, and all of a sudden, I heard a bloodcurdling scream to my right. It was Lucia. She was holding her hands high in the air and screaming at the top of her lungs. She was staring at the buttered noodles with a look of sheer horror; you would have thought they tossed the penne with slugs and puppy dog tails. What, might you imagine, could cause such a visceral reaction? Parsley, the dreaded "green stuff." Some well-meaning, no-children-having line cook decided to be fancy and sprinkled on parsley. Oh, the horror. From then on out, I prefaced all orders for Lucia with "no green stuff." This chili has no green stuff and no beans either—it's Lucia approved.

SERVES 10

3½ tablespoons chili powder

2 pounds ground beef

1 onion, chopped

1 jalapeño, seeded and finely chopped

4 cloves garlic, minced

1 (14.5-ounce) can diced tomatoes, drained

1 red bell pepper, finely chopped

1½ cups beef broth

1 cup beer or cola

1 tablespoon tomato paste

1 tablespoon brown sugar (optional; if using cola, that is all the sweetness you will need)

1 tablespoon ground cumin

Salt and pepper, to taste

1. Sprinkle the chili powder over the ground beef. In a large, heavy pot, brown the ground beef mixture, onion, jalapeño, and garlic, stirring often. Drain off all of the fat.

2. Add the tomatoes, bell pepper, broth, beer, tomato paste, brown sugar (if using), cumin, salt, and pepper to the beef mixture and simmer, uncovered, for at least 45 minutes. You may have to add a little more broth if the chili gets too thick before the 45 minutes is up. Or if you want your chili a little thicker, continue to simmer until the chili has reduced to the desired thickness. Serve, or pack in a thermos or other insulated container.

Mom Tip If your children are not horrified by the sight of a pinto bean, feel free to add two 15-ounce cans beans to this recipe. I just got tired of fishing them out of their chili, so I gave up altogether and don't add them at all.

Old-Fashioned Meat Loaf Sandwiches

———◦◦◦◦◦◦———

Momma used to make us meat loaf sandwiches when we were little, with just three ingredients— ice-cold meat loaf, ketchup, and white bread. I hated them. As soon as Momma walked out of the kitchen, I would quickly shove my sandwich in the linen drawer in the cabinet right behind my chair. I will never forget the horror on my mother's face when she went to get linen napkins for her bridge club and opened the drawer to find my moldy, decomposing meat loaf sandwiches inside.

You'd think that meat loaf was dead to me forever, but I know a good thing when I taste it. This fancy meat loaf sandwich with all the fixins elevates an already great thing—my Old-Fashioned Meat Loaf.

MAKES 4 SANDWICHES

2 tablespoons vegetable oil

1 yellow onion, thinly sliced

Salt

½ cup mayonnaise

3 tablespoons prepared horseradish, drained

2 dashes Worcestershire sauce

¼ teaspoon Cajun seasoning

8 slices whole-grain bread

4 leaves Bibb lettuce

4 slices Old-Fashioned Meat Loaf (recipe follows)

1. In a medium skillet, heat the oil over medium-high heat. Add the onion and a pinch of salt and cook, stirring, until the onion is caramelized, about 13 minutes.

2. In a small bowl, mix the mayonnaise, horseradish, Worcestershire, and Cajun seasoning.

3. To assemble the sandwiches, spread the horseradish mayo on the bread and top with the lettuce, meat loaf, and onion.

OLD-FASHIONED MEAT LOAF

SERVES 4, WITH LEFTOVERS

3 slices white sandwich bread, crusts cut off

6 saltine crackers (or other crackers), crushed

1 cup milk

3 pounds ground beef

½ medium onion, finely chopped

2 large eggs, lightly beaten

8 teaspoons Creole seasoning (preferably Tony Chachere's)

¼ cup ketchup

2 teaspoons freshly ground black pepper

1 teaspoon salt

½ teaspoon hot sauce

3 tablespoons Worcestershire sauce

1. Preheat the oven to 350°F.

2. In a large bowl, combine the bread, saltines, and milk. Let sit for a few minutes for the milk to be absorbed.

3. Add the ground beef, onion, eggs, Creole seasoning, ketchup, pepper, salt, hot sauce, and Worcestershire. Use your clean hands to mix well but gently; if you overwork the meat it will become tough.

4. Line a 9 x 13-inch baking dish with foil. Put the meat mixture in the middle of the baking dish and use your hands to shape it into a loaf. Bake for about 35 minutes.

5. Let cool for at least 10 minutes before slicing and serving. Store leftovers in an airtight container in the refrigerator for up to 4 days.

LEFTOVER
Chicken Pasta

Packing school lunches can be the most challenging culinary task you will face. There are very few recipes that can be made at the crack of dawn, squished by books in a backpack, thrown around for five hours, and then served at slightly lower than room temperature. This pasta salad is up to the task. I cook chicken in some form or fashion at least two nights a week. I always make double the chicken so that I have extra on hand for chicken salad, a quick lunch, or this pasta recipe. Then I cook some penne pasta the night before and throw the chicken in with it. The next morning, I just pour the vinaigrette over the pasta, put it in the lunch box, and off they go.

SERVES 5

Salt and pepper

1 (1-pound) box penne pasta

2 cups baby heirloom tomatoes, halved

2 small zucchini, trimmed, cut in half lengthwise, and thinly sliced into half moons

1 small red bell pepper, cut into thin strips

1 cup fresh corn kernels (from 2 ears), or frozen

2 firm, ripe medium peaches, diced (1 cup)

½ cup thinly sliced green onions (white and green parts)

1 cup Parmesan Vinaigrette (recipe follows)

2 cups shredded or chopped cooked chicken (see Mom Tip, page 33)

1. Bring a large pot of salted water to a boil. Cook the pasta according to the package directions. Drain and let cool slightly.

2. Meanwhile, toss together the tomatoes, zucchini, bell pepper, corn, peaches, green onions, and vinaigrette in a large bowl and let stand for 10 minutes.

3. Add the pasta and chicken to the tomato mixture; toss gently to coat. Season with salt and pepper to taste. Transfer to a platter and serve, or pack in airtight containers for lunch.

PARMESAN VINAIGRETTE

MAKES ABOUT 1½ CUPS

½ cup grated parmesan cheese

½ cup olive oil

2 teaspoons grated lemon zest

3 tablespoons fresh lemon juice (from 1 medium lemon)

1 tablespoon balsamic vinegar

2 cloves garlic, peeled

2 teaspoons pepper

½ teaspoon salt

¼ cup chopped fresh basil

¼ cup chopped fresh cilantro

1. Process the cheese, olive oil, lemon zest, lemon juice, balsamic vinegar, garlic, pepper, and salt in a blender or food processor until smooth. Add the basil and cilantro; pulse 5 or 6 times or just until blended. The dressing will keep in an airtight container in the refrigerator for up to 3 weeks.

PRESSED
Ham Sandwiches

—⦿⦾⦿—

One of the challenges with a lunch-box lunch is that you are handing over this lovely lunch creation to a child to manage for five hours. I can only imagine what happens after they leave the house. I am pretty sure there is a lot of shoving going on—into a desk, a locker, or a backpack. The end result can only be tragic. That's why my kids and I love this pressed ham sandwich. It's already shoved, mashed, and pressed—which forces the vinaigrette into the ciabatta, making it extra delicious. Any future shoving, mashing, or pressing only makes it better.

The key to this sandwich is the bread. A ciabatta that has a tough exterior and soft interior is just perfect, so the bread will soak up the vinaigrette but not turn into a mushy mess. Not only can you make these sandwiches the night before, it's a must.

MAKES 4 LARGE OR 8 SMALL SANDWICHES

¼ cup red wine vinegar

1 teaspoon Cavender's Greek seasoning

½ cup olive oil

1 (12-inch) loaf ciabatta bread, halved horizontally, insides scooped out and discarded

Optional additional toppings: fresh basil leaves, chopped or sliced sun-dried tomatoes, olive tapenade, Dijon mustard, pesto, sliced pickles

1 pound sliced deli ham

4 ounces sliced provolone, swiss, or muenster cheese

1. In a small bowl, combine the vinegar and Greek seasoning, then slowly whisk in the olive oil. Brush the vinaigrette over the cut insides of the ciabatta. If using additional toppings, add these to the bottom half of the ciabatta now.

2. Layer the ham and cheese on the bottom half of the ciabatta; cover with the top half.

3. Wrap the sandwich tightly in plastic wrap and set it on a small cutting board or baking dish. Place a heavy object such as a cast-iron pan, heavy book, or brick on top of the sandwich. Refrigerate overnight or for at least 6 hours.

4. Remove from fridge, cut into individual sandwiches, and serve, or pack for lunch.

Egg Roll
IN A BOWL

I got this recipe from my friend Kristy. She claims she doesn't know how to cook, but she was able to turn a bag of precut slaw, some sausage, and a few other simple ingredients into this very tasty masterpiece she calls "egg roll in a bowl." I quickly put it into my dinner rotation as well. I finally had to start doubling it because the girls wanted to take the leftovers to school the next day. It is just as good cold or at room temperature as it is hot—perfect for the lunch box.

SERVES 4

1 pound bulk pork sausage, ground beef, or ground turkey

6 cups coleslaw mix or shredded green cabbage

1 tablespoon finely chopped peeled fresh ginger

4 cloves garlic, minced

1 tablespoon soy sauce

¼ cup plus 1 tablespoon chopped green onions (white and green parts)

1 tablespoon toasted sesame oil

¼ cup each chopped fresh cilantro, basil, and mint (optional)

1. Heat a large skillet over medium heat; add the sausage and cook, stirring from time to time, until it is crumbled, cooked through, and no longer pink; do not drain.

2. Add the coleslaw, ginger, garlic, and soy sauce; cook until the cabbage wilts a bit. Remove from the heat.

3. Add the green onions, sesame oil, and fresh herbs (if using). Mix well and serve, or pack in airtight containers for lunch. Any leftovers can be stored in an airtight container in the refrigerator for up to 4 days.

"BUNCHABLES"
Taco Boxes

What in the world is the appeal of the Lunchable? I still to this day cannot figure it out. My children would spot the yellow boxes in the grocery store; their eyes would widen and then glaze over as if they were looking at new money. Legs and arms would go flying as they escaped the grocery cart. Full speed ahead to the lunch meat section. Once I caught up with them, I would have to pry the boxes out of their little hands, followed by screaming and tears. If I had handed them three slices of American cheese, three slices of slick turkey, and one cookie on a plate, the girls would have looked at me like I was completely insane. But put it in a box, and the girls couldn't get enough. So I stole this approach, using containers with multiple little compartments to make healthy (and more delicious) lunches. If you are wondering if this stopped all the drama at the Kroger, it didn't. But at least now the fight was in the cereal aisle.

SERVES 1

4 ounces grilled chicken or steak, shredded or chopped (about ½ cup)

1 tablespoon sour cream

2 tablespoons salsa

3 tablespoons shredded cheddar cheese

4 cherry tomatoes, chopped

2 corn tortillas

1. Divide the ingredients into the compartments of a lunch box or bento box, or multiple small containers; snap the lid on tight and send to school. Let your child build their own tacos at lunch.

FROZEN FRUIT
Smoothies

This lunch-box treat hits all the high notes. You can make it ahead, it thaws beautifully, and it will help keep all the other items in the lunch box nice and chilly. I started making these when I just couldn't bear to make another sandwich. And if I couldn't make another sandwich, the girls probably didn't want to eat another one, either. At first, I would get up super early to load all the fresh fruit into the blender and begin making batches of smoothies; then into the thermos they would go. Then I got smart. Why not make them the night before, put them in the freezer, and sleep in that extra hour? Now I have even eliminated the need to have a separate cold pack on top of it all. No more sandwiches, the kids are happy, and I get to sleep; win, win, win!

SERVES 4

2 cups frozen peaches, strawberries, blueberries, or raspberries, or a mix

1 banana

½ cup almond milk or coconut milk beverage

½ cup vanilla Greek yogurt

1 tablespoon honey or agave syrup, or more to taste

1. Put all the ingredients in the blender and blend until smooth. Pour into four (8-ounce) plastic freezer jars with screw top lids. Freeze at least 3 hours. Pack and let thaw in the lunch box.

Mom Tip If you travel a lot and are always in an airport you know the food choices are limited at best. I love a smoothie but you can't bring one through security because it's a liquid. Unless you freeze it. By the time you board the plane, it will have thawed and you have a super healthy meal.

Chicken and Ranch Wraps

There really ought to be a manual on how to raise children. Okay, I know there are probably 1,000 on the market already. But I am talking about one with advice that I could have used—real world, practical advice. For example, if it's time to leave the McDonald's PlayPlace and your child is at the top of the enclosed playhouse and refuses to come out? Do not lose your mind and try to climb up the tube slide to drag them out. You will not fit, you will get stuck, and the manager will have to come and pull you by the feet to get your body unwedged. These are the things that I needed to know. Another thing: If you have a picky eater, don't make a fuss. Don't threaten the child, and don't put the child in time out; just put some ranch on it. Problem solved. This lunch-box wrap is a tasty treat your kids will absolutely love.

MAKES 4 WRAPS

4 (8-inch) flour tortillas

2 cups shredded or sliced cooked chicken
(see Mom Tip, page 33)

½ cup shredded mozzarella cheese

¼ cup fresh spinach

½ cucumber, thinly sliced

¼ cup homemade or store-bought ranch
dressing

1. Lay the tortillas on your counter. Divide the chicken, cheese, spinach, and cucumber between them, making sure to leave a 1-inch border all the way around the edges. Drizzle with the ranch dressing. Roll up the wraps burrito-style; wrap tightly in foil or plastic wrap; pack for lunch or chill in the fridge for up to 3 hours (or serve immediately).

Yogurt Parfaits

———◆◇◇◇◇◆———

After raising kids for twenty-one years, there are a few things that I know for sure. Children will put anything up their noses; a bag of Oreos can stop a screaming fit on a dime; and when kids can help prepare their own food, they will happily eat every bite. Kids are hardly any different than adults. They like choices, they like to be in control, and they like to be independent.

Yogurt is high in protein, a great source of calcium, and low in sugar, making it a really healthy breakfast or lunch option. Now, plain yogurt might not be the most appealing food to a kid. On the other hand, plain yogurt with a wide assortment of toppings to mix in or layer on top, well, it's a game changer. When making the girls' lunches, I would put the yogurt in insulated containers to keep it super cold.

Have fun with these toppings; this recipe is merely meant to be a guide. You can also make the seasoned yogurt ahead of time and store it (without the toppings) in the refrigerator for a couple days.

SERVES 4

1 quart plain Greek yogurt

3 tablespoons honey

½ teaspoon vanilla extract

1 teaspoon grated orange zest

Suggested toppings: granola, dried coconut, dried fruit such as berries or chopped apricots, chopped fresh fruit, chocolate chips, assorted nuts, white chocolate chunks

1. In a large bowl, mix the yogurt, honey, vanilla, and orange zest. To serve, layer the yogurt with the desired toppings in bowls or glasses. To pack for later, put the yogurt mixture and toppings into separate small containers.

Turkey Spinach Meatballs

I feel like a broken record when I say that you can double this recipe, freeze half, and still have leftovers for lunch. But I am repeating myself because I know that you all don't have any more time than I do. Having meatballs in the freezer is like having good insurance. There will come a day when you are so behind and you don't think you will ever catch up. Even on the most hectic and stressful days, you will still have a hungry family that has to eat. Pull out these meatballs, make a pot of pasta, and pour on a jar of store-bought marinara. Dinner is served in the time it would take you to get through a drive-through. But these are also a great alternative to boring, worn-out PB & J sandwiches for lunch. They can be eaten hot, cold, or somewhere in between. For a surefire way to make sure your kids eat them, put them on a toothpick. I will never understand why, but when I gave my kids food on a toothpick, I knew every morsel would be eaten. Happy plates all around!

SERVES 6 TO 8

1 (10-ounce) package frozen chopped spinach, thawed and drained

1¼ pounds ground turkey

1 large egg, beaten

½ cup finely chopped onion (about ½ onion)

¼ cup grated parmesan cheese

2 cloves garlic, minced

1 teaspoon dried oregano

1 teaspoon dried basil

2 teaspoons salt

1 teaspoon pepper

1. Preheat the oven to 350°F and line a rimmed baking sheet with foil.

2. Place the spinach in a fine-mesh strainer and press to remove as much liquid as possible. Gather the spinach into a ball and squeeze to remove even more moisture. (This step is critical to making sure the meatballs bind properly.) Transfer the spinach to a large bowl.

3. Add the turkey, egg, onion, parmesan cheese, garlic, oregano, basil, salt, and pepper to the spinach and mix gently. (Your clean hands are the best tool for mixing.) Be careful not to overwork the meat. You want the meatballs to be tender.

4. Roll the meatball mixture into golf ball–size portions and place on the prepared baking sheet. Bake for 20 to 25 minutes, until the meatballs are no longer pink in the center and an instant-read thermometer inserted in a meatball reads 165°F. Serve, or let cool and pack in airtight containers for lunch.

When it comes to
eating healthy,
I've got you covered

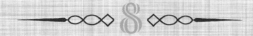

DIET DAYS

There is not one diet that I haven't been on, honey! I have a recipe for every single diet in existence, so when it comes to eating healthy, I've got you covered. I love a diet. Every one of them offers such hope and promise. It's new and exciting and this one by God is going to work. I went on my first diet when I was eleven years old. That would be the Scarsdale Diet—grapefruit, stewed tomatoes, and cold cuts. Fourteen pounds in fourteen days was the promise. The torture ended at 1:30 p.m. on the second day.

Out of all the diets I've been on over the years, these recipes are a few tasty keepers.

BLTA Salad

BLTs have always been that one sandwich that I just cannot get enough of. I don't know if it's the smoky bacon, the toasted, buttered white bread, or the mayonnaise that mixes with the juices from the tomato that makes my heart leap with joy. I started adding avocado to this sandwich after a trip to New York City in the '90s. In my hotel, I called down to the kitchen and proceeded to make my standard room service order: a BLT, chips, and a Coke. (I never look at a room service menu because any respectable hotel has a BLT, or at the very least, a club sandwich. When you are far from home and maybe a little lonely, a BLT comforts like nothing else.) When I placed my order, the waiter asked if I would like avocado on my BLT. I could have sworn I heard the angels singing. Hell, yes, I want the avocado. When I went on a keto diet, sandwiches were not an option, so I started making this simple salad using the same ingredients. Adding some shrimp or chicken makes it an amazing light supper.

SERVES 4

6 cups chopped romaine lettuce
(about 1 head)

2 very ripe tomatoes (preferably heirloom),
chopped

2 avocados, pitted and cut into chunks

8 slices bacon, cooked crisp and cut into
½-inch pieces (you want to be able to see
and taste the bacon)

½ cup crumbled goat cheese or blue cheese,
or shaved or shredded parmesan cheese

½ to 1 cup Disappearing Vinaigrette
(page 212)

1. In a large salad bowl, combine the lettuce, tomatoes, avocado, bacon, and cheese. Drizzle with enough vinaigrette to coat the lettuce and other ingredients. Give the salad a good toss; you want the tomatoes to release their juices and the avocados to lend their creamy texture to the lettuce. Serve immediately.

Fat Lady Soup

The Charleston Wine and Food Festival is a weekend of overindulgence on every level. Everywhere you turn, there is some amazing morsel to try, a twelve-course dinner under the live oaks, or a BBQ with forty of the best pitmasters in the South. I am weak and have a hard time saying no; I generally act like I've been let out of a box. The first time I was invited to attend this food festival, I stayed with my good friends Chris and Libba. We went from one event to another, hardly sobering up to get to the next party. After the weekend was done, on the way to the airport, Libba called her sister, Caroline, and explained we had been at Charleston Wine and Food all weekend and that she needed the Fat Lady Soup recipe. After she got off the phone, Libba told me that she and Caroline would eat nothing but this soup after a weekend of debauchery. It was a self-imposed detox they had gotten from their mother. Now it is also my go-to to get back on track after overindulging, the righter of all wrongdoings.

SERVES 6

3 tablespoons olive oil

1 large onion, finely chopped

4 cloves garlic, minced

4 large carrots, peeled and cut into 1-inch pieces

5 stalks celery, cut into small dice

1 red bell pepper, cut into small dice

12 ounces fresh green beans, ends removed, cut into 1-inch pieces (2 cups)

1 (28-ounce) can diced tomatoes

1 (8-ounce) can tomato sauce

8 cups vegetable or chicken broth

½ head green cabbage, shredded and cut into 1-inch pieces

½ cup chopped fresh parsley

1 teaspoon dried oregano

1 teaspoon dried basil

½ teaspoon dried thyme

Salt and pepper

1. In a large soup pot, heat the oil over medium heat. Sauté the onion and garlic until soft and translucent, about 3 minutes.

2. Add the carrots, celery, bell pepper, and green beans. Cook for 10 to 15 minutes.

3. Stir in the tomatoes with their juices and the tomato sauce. Add the broth, cabbage, parsley, oregano, basil, and thyme. Reduce the heat to a simmer and cook until the cabbage is tender but not mushy. Season with salt and pepper to taste.

4. You can serve this soup immediately, or cool and freeze it so you have it on hand during a detox emergency. It lasts up to 5 days in an airtight container in the fridge, up to 3 months frozen.

MEDITERRANEAN
Chopped Salad

This recipe is one that I fell in love with while doing the Perricone Diet. This anti-inflammatory diet not only offered the promise of weight loss, but also the side effect of magnificent glowing skin. Well, count me in! (And yes, it worked!) I would make this salad up by the boatload and keep it in the fridge for lunch, dinner, and snacks. It's excellent topped with grilled chicken, shrimp, or salmon.

SERVES 6

1 cucumber, peeled and cut into ¼-inch dice

1 red bell pepper, cut into ¼-inch dice

3 stalks celery, cut into ¼-inch dice

1 cup cherry tomatoes, quartered

2 tablespoons chopped red onion

2 tablespoons finely chopped fresh parsley

1 tablespoon fresh lemon juice

6 black olives, pitted and quartered

2 ounces feta cheese, crumbled
(about ¼ cup)

2 tablespoons extra virgin olive oil

4 cups fresh arugula, heavy stems removed

2 cups cooked quinoa, room temperature

1. Mix all the ingredients together in a large nonmetallic bowl. Serve immediately, or cover and store in the refrigerator for up to 3 days.

Bone Broth

The bone broth diet popular a few years ago promised·glowing skin, healthy hair, and strong nails. I would call my local butcher, the Neon Pig, and buy bags of bones, then cook them down in not one but three slow cookers for days on end. At the height of the diet, I was buying three bags per week. I know the guys at the Pig were talking about me and they would get a worried look on their faces when I'd walk in to fetch my bones. The whole plan was pretty simple: you ate a diet of low-carb, high-fat foods one day and consumed nothing but bone broth the next day. I think I lasted about two weeks. To tell you the truth, I still have two quarts of bone broth in my freezer. But that's okay because even if you are not on a diet, it is a fabulous broth for making soup.

MAKES 3 QUARTS BROTH, ABOUT 8 SERVINGS

3 to 4 pounds beef, chicken, or pork bones (chicken feet also work very well)

2 tablespoons apple cider vinegar

1 large onion, chopped

3 carrots, peeled and chopped

3 stalks celery, chopped

4 cloves garlic, not peeled, crushed with the flat side of a knife

½ cup chopped fresh parsley

2 teaspoons salt

1 teaspoon whole black peppercorns

6 fresh thyme sprigs

4 or 5 slices fresh ginger (no need to peel it), plus ½ teaspoon grated peeled fresh ginger

3 bay leaves

3 tablespoons soy sauce

2 tablespoons toasted sesame oil

1. Place the bones, vinegar, onion, carrots, celery, garlic, parsley, salt, peppercorns, thyme, ginger slices, and bay leaves in a slow cooker. Add enough water to cover. Cook on low heat for 24 to 48 hours. You will know it is done when the bones have no more marrow and there is no meat or connective tissue still attached.

2. Remove the bones and strain the broth through a fine-mesh strainer into a large bowl or another pot; make sure to press the vegetables into the strainer to release all their flavor and liquid.

3. After the broth is strained, add the soy sauce, sesame oil, and grated ginger; taste and adjust the seasonings. Try not to add too much salt or soy sauce because sodium can make you retain water. (The whole point of enduring this is to watch the scale go down!) Store in the fridge in airtight containers for up to 5 days or freeze for up to 6 months.

"BLAND AND BORING"
Turkey Soup

The turkey diet went like this: You got to eat every three hours. (I loved that part.) You only ate protein shakes, chicken, broccoli, turkey, and eggs. I hated that part of the diet—no beer, no wine, no fruit, no nothing. I got so tired of chicken and turkey I wanted to scream. I decided to come up with a soup just to change things up a bit. You can take liberties with this by adding herbs and other veggies. I still will drag this recipe out if I need to get back on track after eating unhealthfully. It is also a low- to no-calorie snack that will surprisingly fill you up, but for only about 10 minutes.

SERVES 8

2 pounds ground turkey (85/15 is good, 93/7 is better)

½ onion, chopped

4 cloves garlic, minced

2 stalks celery, chopped

8 cups chicken broth

2 bay leaves

½ teaspoon dried thyme

1 head broccoli, cut into pieces small enough to fit in a spoon

4 cups fresh spinach leaves

½ cup chopped fresh parsley

½ cup chopped fresh basil leaves

1. In a heavy-bottomed soup pot, cook the turkey over medium heat, stirring often, until crumbled, thoroughly done, and no longer pink, 5 to 7 minutes; do not drain.

2. Add the onion, garlic, and celery and cook until the onion is softened and translucent, about 3 minutes.

3. Add the chicken broth, bay leaves, and thyme. Bring to a boil and then reduce the heat to a simmer for 10 minutes. Add the broccoli, spinach, parsley, and basil; continue to simmer for 7 minutes more, until the broccoli is tender.

4. Remove the bay leaves and serve immediately, or let cool and store in the fridge for up to 5 days. The soup also freezes beautifully.

DISAPPEARING
Vinaigrette

My father made the dressing I am about to share with you almost every night for thirty years. We had a beautiful wooden salad bowl. He would smash garlic in the bottom of the bowl, sprinkle salt and pepper over it, and then, with the back of a fork, mash the garlic into the salt and pepper, making sure all the juices from the garlic were released. Then a little dry mustard, freshly squeezed lemon juice, and finally the oil, whisked in with a fork.

There really is no reason to buy bottled, processed salad dressing; it couldn't be any simpler to make. One part acid to three parts oil. The acid can be any one you like—cider vinegar or balsamic vinegar; lemon, lime, or grapefruit juice. The oil can be canola oil, olive oil, grapeseed oil, or even pecan oil. You also need to add a little Dijon mustard or dry mustard to your mix. Mustard acts like the marriage counselor: It helps hold two things together that do not want to stay together—the oil and the acid. It is a great binder. The last and most important trick is to make sure you slowly drizzle the oil into your acid.

My dad's salad was always simple: lettuce, tomatoes, and avocados. On rare occasions, he would add blue cheese; it really was all about the dressing.

MAKES 1½ CUPS

3 cloves garlic, chopped

Salt and pepper

¼ teaspoon dry mustard

¼ cup fresh lemon juice

1 cup good-quality olive oil

1. Place the garlic in the bottom of a salad bowl; sprinkle with the salt and pepper and mash with a fork to release all the garlic's juices. Stir in the dry mustard and then the lemon juice.

2. Slowly drizzle the olive oil into the bowl, whisking vigorously until the olive oil and lemon juice are thoroughly combined. Serve over your favorite salad or store in a mason jar in the fridge for up to 3 months.

Chef Tip All vinaigrette recipes say to slowly drizzle in the oil. They didn't add this sentence because they needed more words in the recipe. It really is that important: Whisking and slowly drizzling the oil makes the difference between a broken vinaigrette and one that is beautifully emulsified.

VINAIGRETTE MAKES IT ALL BETTER

I feel like I am an expert on dieting. I have been on a diet since I was in the fifth grade. If I know one thing, it's that if the food doesn't taste good, you are less likely to stay on the diet. Steamed veggies and no butter, yuck. Plain boneless, skinless chicken breast, yuck. I started making big batches of vinaigrettes, storing them in the fridge, and drizzling them over any diet recipe that would otherwise be bland and boring. Try this trick and I promise the weight will disappear.

Shaved Carrot and Walnut Salad

When Luke and I first started the farm, I was most excited about growing carrots. After all, I had been reading about them growing in Mr. McGregor's garden in Beatrix Potter books since childhood. We grew the most beautiful baby carrots you have ever seen. As the season went on, sometimes carrots would be left to grow larger; then there were those that would be overlooked completely. The results were completely mind-boggling: When the forgotten carrots were dug up, they would be as big as Luke's foot. There wasn't a chef in the world that would buy them from us! So instead I created this carrot salad with walnuts and currants. It is very reminiscent of the salad our lunch ladies at the Presbyterian Day School made on hotdog day. Theirs had mayo, shaved carrots, and raisins. I have to say, and please forgive me Miss Arleen and Miss Vance, this one is a whole lot better! I have served this salad at lovely dinner parties as a delicious and beautiful first course. I have also whipped it up in the kitchen on diet days. It also happens to be paleo, although it honestly tastes so good you would never know it. Of course, if you're not on a diet, you can always add a little blue cheese, too.

**SERVES 5 AS A FIRST COURSE
OR 2 AS A MAIN COURSE**

10 large carrots, shaved with a vegetable peeler

1 fennel bulb, thinly sliced

2 cups toasted walnuts

2 apples, thinly sliced

2 cucumbers, shaved into long ribbons with a vegetable peeler

½ cup Disappearing Vinaigrette (page 212)

Salt and pepper

1. Mix the carrots, fennel, walnuts, apples, and cucumbers in a large bowl. Pour enough of the vinaigrette over the vegetables and nuts to coat but not drown them; toss to coat. Season with salt and pepper to taste and serve.

Kale Yes Juice

I have never been good at moderation. I am all in or all out on the wagon, or in the ditch; no in-between. I love the idea of a quick-fix fifteen pounds in thirty days. A juice cleanse is one of the many quick fixes I've tried. It's a pretty simple concept: nothing but pressed juices. That's it, all liquid for as long as you can stand it. The good news is, my husband and I operate a farm; during the time I tried this juice cleanse, kale was growing like a weed. Crates and crates of kale abounded. This was excellent because it damn near takes a crate of kale to make one cup of juice. I would get up at the crack of dawn to make all my juices for the day. The kitchen looked like a farmers' market. Everyone in the house was furious with me because no one wants to be woken up by the sound of a screaming juicer at 5:00 a.m. (And yes, you will need a juicer to make this recipe.) I would carefully pour all of juices into mason jars, pack them in a cooler, and my day was done. If a hunger pang struck, I drank a juice. If I was light-headed from hunger, I drank a juice. If I was about to pass out from hunger, I drank a juice. I did this for eight days. Did the weight come off? Yes. Did it also come back? Yes!

Now, while a full-on 100 percent juice cleanse is not a good idea, I do think it's good to let your digestive system rest every now and then. And I still drink this delicious green juice on occasion.

MAKES 2½ CUPS

4 bunches kale

2 Granny Smith apples

4 cucumbers

1 lemon

1. Wash the kale well, making sure to remove all the sand and dirt; it's important to wash each leaf individually. Cut the apples into 8 pieces; no need to core them. Cut the cucumbers into 2-inch pieces; peel the lemon and discard the peels, or if your knife skills are lacking, squeeze the juice from the lemon.

2. Feed the first bunch of kale into your juicer; follow with a little apple, then cucumber to help push the kale through. Continue until the apples, kale, and cucumbers are finished.

3. If you peeled the lemon, add it to the juicer; if not, add the squeezed lemon juice to the processed juice.

4. Pour into mason jars, screw on the lids, and chill in the fridge or enjoy immediately.

Ginger Avocado Salad

There are just some people in this world that are especially stunning and so beautiful, you just cannot take your eyes off of them. Their beauty is effortless. Even without makeup and no blow-out; no creams, potions, or salves. They are sheer perfection. Everyone wants to look like them and be like them. Whatever they say they do to attain this beauty, we will try it. It's the Gwyneth Paltrow effect. Gwyneth's blog, goop, inspired me to try a post-holiday detox. Within minutes, I was pulling out my juicer and googling ingredients I had never heard of, all because Gwyneth told me to. This recipe is one of the holdovers from that three-day detox. It is exceptionally delicious and I still eat it frequently, diet or no diet. Finger food can be a lot more fun than a garden-variety tossed salad, so I like to serve this in little lettuce cups. But you could chop the lettuce and toss everything together if you like.

SERVES 4

For the Dressing

1 large carrot, peeled and coarsely chopped

1 large shallot, coarsely chopped

2 tablespoons coarsely chopped peeled fresh ginger

2 tablespoons rice vinegar

1 tablespoon sweet white miso

1 tablespoon toasted sesame oil

¼ cup grapeseed oil or other neutral-tasting oil

For the Salad

1 head baby gem lettuce or other greens, leaves separated

¼ red onion, thinly sliced

¼ avocado, pitted, peeled, and finely diced

1. **MAKE THE DRESSING:** Combine the carrot, shallot, and ginger in a blender or food processor and pulse until finely chopped. Scrape down the sides and add the vinegar, miso, and sesame oil, then blend together until smooth. With the blender going, slowly drizzle in the oil. Add up to 2 tablespoons water a little at a time if the dressing seems too thick.

2. **ASSEMBLE THE SALAD:** Combine the onion and avocado in a large bowl. Nestle the avocado mixture in the lettuce leaves on a serving platter or on individual plates. Drizzle with plenty of dressing and serve.

At some point,
you just
have to let loose

9

CHEAT DAYS

Before I start a diet I have one hell of a cheat day! After all, you have to get rid of all the temptation in the cabinet. I say, make an amazing shake with all the leftover cookies, cupcakes, and candy in the house for one last hurrah before the dreaded diet begins.

I can white-knuckle through the worst diets known to man. To be honest, I would eat cold steel if I thought it would help me lose a pound. But you can cry yourself to sleep only so many nights remembering the amazing pasta dish you turned down to eat cauliflower rice for the thousandth time. An epic weekend of cheat days is sure to follow. At some point, you just have to let loose and allow yourself to fall off the wagon. But don't worry, there is always hope in the next diet.

Brie Pasta

If I was only able to eat one food for the rest of my life it would be cheese—or maybe a toss-up between cheese and pasta. Thank goodness I don't have to choose. This recipe is the height of indulgence. Put on the fat pants and get ready to feast!

SERVES 8

1 (35-ounce) wheel Brie cheese

Salt

1½ pounds spaghetti noodles

2 tablespoons extra virgin olive oil

3 cloves garlic, minced

¼ cup chopped fresh parsley

1 pinch red pepper flakes

4 slices thick-cut bacon, cooked and cut into ½-inch pieces (reserve the grease for another another use)

¼ cup grated parmesan cheese

1. Preheat the oven to 350°F. Cut off the top rind of the Brie and place the wheel in an ovenproof skillet—cast iron is best—about its same size. Bake until the Brie is bubbling and totally melted throughout, about 25 minutes.

2. Meanwhile, bring a large pot of salted water to a boil. Cook the spaghetti according to the package instructions. Drain the spaghetti and transfer it to a large bowl.

3. Toss the spaghetti with the olive oil, garlic, parsley, and red pepper flakes. Add the bacon. Season with salt to taste.

4. After removing the Brie from the oven, immediately add one serving of spaghetti to the Brie in the skillet and toss until coated, using tongs; transfer to a serving bowl. Repeat until all serving bowls are filled. Serve immediately, sprinkled with the parmesan.

BLUEBERRY
French Toast Casserole

————◦⬦◦————

Blueberry french toast is the best way I can think of to greet a new day. My alarm goes off at 5:00 a.m., five days a week. Off to yoga I go; my weeks are very structured and I usually cater on Saturday nights. By the time Sunday comes, I am ready to relax. This blueberry french toast is an amazing way to celebrate Sunday. You can assemble it on Friday or Saturday and let it sit in the fridge. It actually does better because all that yummy goodness has time to really soak into the bread. Blueberry season in Mississippi is long and plentiful. I will go to the farmers' market to stock up and will eat half in the car on the way home. I put them in salads, on cereal, in smoothies, and in this delicious french toast.

SERVES 10 TO 12

Butter, for greasing the baking dish

1 large loaf day-old French bread or brioche

8 large eggs

5 cups half-and-half

⅓ cup granulated sugar

2 teaspoons ground cinnamon

2 teaspoons vanilla extract

½ teaspoon salt

1 cup fresh blueberries, tossed with
1 tablespoon all-purpose flour (to stop them from turning the french toast purple)

8 ounces cream cheese, cut into 1-inch chunks

Powdered sugar (optional), for dusting

1. Butter a 9 x 13-inch baking dish. Cut the bread into 2-inch chunks and set aside.

2. In a large bowl, gently beat the eggs. Add the half-and-half, granulated sugar, cinnamon, vanilla, and salt; whisk until the sugar is dissolved. Add the bread, berries, and cream cheese and mix gently. Pour into the prepared baking dish.

3. Cover the baking dish with foil and refrigerate overnight or for at least 4 hours so the bread chunks can absorb the custard.

4. Preheat the oven to 350°F. Uncover the baking dish and bake for about 45 minutes, until the middle is set and all the custard is absorbed. If the top gets too brown before the casserole is done, cover it with foil. Dust with powdered sugar, if using, and serve immediately.

Summer Beer

When we moved our family to Oxford, Mississippi, seven years ago, I was just beside myself. You would have thought we had moved to a foreign country. We were only an hour away from my beloved Delta but it felt like a million miles. It wasn't until I reconnected with a few old friends from the Delta that I started to feel more at home. My group of Delta transplants threw a welcome party for Luke and me. I didn't want to drink too much that night; I wanted to make a good first impression. I thought the summer beer they served was just beer watered down with lemonade. How much trouble could that get me in? Well, one key component I didn't know about was the vodka. I had one and I was fine; one more and I was a little loose. One more and I was as loose as a goose! Summer beer is one of those things that sneaks up on you. Proceed with caution!

SERVES 6

4 (12-ounce) bottles Corona or any lite beer or lager

2 (12-ounce) cans peach Fresca

1 (12-ounce) can frozen pink lemonade concentrate

¾ lemonade concentrate can vodka (about 1 cup)

Juice of 2 lemons

Lemon slices, for serving

2 cups fresh raspberries

1. In a large pitcher, mix the beer, Fresca, lemonade, vodka, and lemon juice. Serve over ice and garnish with lemon slices and raspberries.

PIMENTO CHEESE–STUFFED
Burgers

My father in-law, Mike, was a legend and I am so lucky to have had him in my life. He loved to have fun, loved to laugh, and loved to eat great food. He is partly responsible for this recipe. Well, him and chef Daniel Boulud. Mike was watching the *TODAY* show one morning and Chef Boulud was on making a burger—but not just any burger, one that started with a ground-up brisket. Not long after that, Mike had his butcher grind up a brisket. The resulting burger was by far the best burger we had ever had. It was tender, juicy, and just amazing. Now we don't do any other kind of burger.

I have always found great value in a little lagniappe. Lagniappe is a Creole term for something extra. I cannot think of a more extra way to complete a burger but to stuff it with pimento cheese and top it with Tater Tots. You just have to remember a few things: First, don't overstuff the burger. Yes, I know it's hard to resist. You want as much of that cheesy goodness as you possibly can get. But if you overstuff it you will end up with a big fat mess. Then, make sure you really seal the edges of the burger. Pimento cheese inside the burger is awesome. Pimento cheese oozing on the grill is not so awesome. Now, on the Tater Tots: deep-fried Tater Tots are really perfection but I can tell you I haven't ever refused a baked one. Whichever cooking method you choose, just know that topping this burger with tots will make you a rock star.

SERVES 4

For the Pimento Cheese

2 cups shredded white cheddar cheese

1 cup mayonnaise

½ cup shredded parmesan cheese

¾ cup roasted red bell peppers (half a 12-ounce jar), drained and diced

¼ cup chopped pecans

¼ cup finely chopped green onions (white and green parts)

¼ teaspoon hot sauce, preferably Tabasco sauce

¼ teaspoon Creole seasoning (preferably Tony Chachere's)

¼ teaspoon Worcestershire sauce

For the Burgers

1¼ pounds ground beef (preferably coarsely ground brisket; ask your butcher to do this)

1 large egg, lightly beaten

¼ cup finely chopped onion

2 tablespoons ketchup

½ teaspoon garlic salt

¼ teaspoon pepper

For Serving

4 hamburger buns

4 slices bacon, cooked crisp (reserve the grease for another use)

Bread and butter pickles, lettuce leaves, tomato slices, and 1 (28-ounce) package Tater Tots, cooked according to package instructions, plus condiments of your choice

1. **MAKE THE PIMENTO CHEESE:** In a large bowl, mix together the cheddar, mayonnaise, parmesan, red peppers, pecans, green onions, hot sauce, Creole seasoning, and Worcestershire until well combined.

2. **MAKE THE BURGERS:** Preheat the grill to medium-high heat.

3. In a large bowl, gently mix together the beef, egg, onion, ketchup, garlic salt, and pepper. Divide the meat mixture into four portions. Then separate each portion in half to form two thin patties for each burger.

4. For each burger, place 2 tablespoons of the pimento cheese in center of one patty. Top with the other patty and press the edges to seal.

5. Grill the patties for 5 to 8 minutes per side, turning once. Remove from the grill and let sit for 5 minutes.

6. **SERVE THE BURGERS** on the buns with the bacon, pickles, lettuce, tomato, Tater Tots, and condiments.

RO*TEL CREAM CHEESE
Sausage Dip

————◇◇◇◇————

The perfect cheat day involves me, some tortilla chips, a couch, and this dip.

SERVES 6

1 pound bulk pork breakfast sausage

1 pound ground beef

4 (10-ounce) cans Ro*Tel tomatoes

4 (8-ounce) packages cream cheese, room temperature

1. In a large pot, cook the sausage and beef together, stirring frequently, until they're well crumbled and no longer pink. Set a large fine-mesh strainer over a bowl, pour in the contents of the pot, and drain off the grease. (Dispose of the grease in the trash.)

2. Return the meat to the pot. Add the tomatoes and their juices and the cream cheese. Cook, stirring frequently, until the cream cheese is melted, being careful not to let it burn on the bottom of the pot. Transfer to a serving bowl and serve warm. This recipe also works great in a slow cooker; brown the meat in a pot as described in step 1, then transfer to a slow cooker and cook on high for 4 hours or low for 8.

WINE AND CHEESE
Grilled Cheese

Two of my most favorite things in the world are wine and cheese. Okay, well, wine, cheese, and beer. Oh, alright! Wine, cheese, beer, and ice cream. And pizza . . . but wine and cheese are at the top of the list. I came up with this recipe while working on a segment for National Wine Day on the *TODAY* show. I was doing the ten o'clock hour with Kathie Lee and Hoda, two ladies who love their wine, so I knew it had to be a great recipe. When I pitched this sandwich, I could hear the producer getting excited from NYC to Mississippi! I know it sounds a little strange, okay a lot strange, but just trust me on this—think about how much you love to eat cheese while drinking wine. Wine grilled cheese is a stroke of pure genius; and yes, Kathie Lee and Hoda approved.

SERVES 4

7 ounces cheddar cheese, cut into 1-inch cubes

2 ounces Brie cheese, rind removed

2 tablespoons dry white wine

2 tablespoons finely chopped shallots

3 tablespoons salted butter, softened

1½ teaspoons whole-grain mustard

8 slices hearty bread

1. Preheat the oven to 425°F. Place two rimmed baking sheets in the oven to heat up for 10 minutes.

2. While the baking sheets are heating, process the cheddar, Brie, and wine in a food processor until they form a smooth paste, 20 to 30 seconds. Add the shallots and pulse to combine.

3. Combine the butter and mustard in a small bowl.

4. Carefully remove the hot baking sheets from the oven. Spread the cheese mixture on four slices of the bread and cover with the remaining slices. Spread the butter mixture on one side of each sandwich and place it buttered side down on a hot baking sheet. Butter the remaining side of each sandwich and cover all the sandwiches with the second hot baking sheet. Place the sandwiched baking sheets in the oven and bake for 15 minutes, until the cheese is melted and the bread is toasted.

BOOZY MILKSHAKES

I had my first dessert from Justine's, a Memphis classic that opened its doors in 1940, at the age of 12. Justine's was sophisticated and elegant, and we often dined there on special occasions. They were famous for so many of their dishes, but the dessert I ate that day, brandy blended with ice cream, will forever be my most favorite. I trace my love affair with boozy milkshakes to that very table so many years ago, although I love them so much that I will only let myself have one now and then.

BOOZY

BOOZY
Caramel-Coffee
MILKSHAKE

MAKES 2 MILKSHAKES

1 cup heavy cream

½ teaspoon vanilla extract

2 tablespoons powdered sugar

4 scoops coffee ice cream (about 2 cups total)

½ cup milk

½ teaspoon espresso powder

1 ounce whiskey, or more if you like it strong

½ cup caramel sauce

¼ cup toffee bits

1. In a stand mixer fitted with the whisk attachment, or in a large bowl using a hand mixer, combine the heavy cream, vanilla, and powdered sugar. Whip, starting on low speed, then increasing the speed as it thickens, until stiff peaks form. Set aside.

2. In a blender, combine the ice cream, milk, espresso powder, and whiskey. Blend until thick and creamy.

3. Drizzle about 2 tablespoons of the caramel sauce on the sides of each milkshake glass. Divide the milkshake between the glasses and top with the remaining caramel sauce, the toffee bits, and whipped cream.

BOOZY

BOOZY
Brandy-Vanilla
MILKSHAKE

MAKES 2 MILKSHAKES

2 cups vanilla ice cream (about 4 scoops)

7 tablespoons brandy

½ cup white crème de cacao

Maraschino cherries, for garnish

1. Combine the ice cream, brandy, and crème de cacao in a blender and blend until smooth.

2. Serve immediately, garnished with maraschino cherries.

ACKNOWLEDGMENTS

To Luke—I wish I had the words that my heart wants me to say. Thank you for supporting all my dreams and believing in me even when I didn't believe in myself. Your encouragement has made all the difference and for that I am deeply grateful.

Stott, Mary Paxton, and Lucia—I am so deeply proud of the women you all are becoming. God blessed me beyond anything I could ever deserve when he brought you three into our lives.

Sarah Virden—This book is as much yours as it is mine. I don't know where I would be without your sound advice, graceful spirit, and grateful heart. God knew I needed a sister and Lord knows you were well worth the wait! Tremendous gratitude to you.

Debbie—I will forever be grateful that you took a chance on this girl from Mississippi. Your believing in me changed everything. Thank you for your love and friendship

Angie—Thank you for pouring all the passion you have to give into each photo. Thank you for loving and caring for this book as if it was your own. Your photos make this book come alive. I value your talent, brilliance, and your dedication but most of all I value your friendship.

Thom—I don't remember when I have fallen so head over heels in love with someone. Your attention to detail and persistence until perfection. Your energy, humor,

and immense talent were truly overwhelming. I will forever be grateful. Thank you for being the best prop stylist, make-up consultant, wardrobe consultant, counselor, hairstylist, and comedian a girl could ask for. Party's over, Steven.

Maddie—Thank you for your passion for this book and the long hours making the food look amazing!

Katherine—Thank you for telling me I was ready to do this. I could hear the words you had spoken to me over the last two books, guiding me each step of the way.

Stacy—Thank you for your expert guidance through this exciting process. You are smart, tough, and experienced. I am lucky to have you as my agent.

Stephanie—Thank you for your ability to turn my horrible grammar and misspelled words into a book I am so deeply proud of. Thank you for your patience and your kindness.

Jessica and Hayden—Thank you for opening your home and your hearts to me. Your giving spirit and generosity is beyond measure. It sure was fun pretending to be Jessica for a few days.

Nicole—Your cabin at Darden was the perfect backdrop for a summer day. I am deeply grateful to you for sharing your special place with not only me but also this book.

Machelle and Ernie—Thank you for letting me use your home as if it was my own. You all are the epitome of hospitality. Your ability to make everyone you come in contact with feel welcomed and wanted is admirable.

Dockery Farms and Bill Lester—This Delta landmark was the perfect backdrop for Delta Days. Thank you for all your efforts to preserve the past so the future can enjoy it.

Amanda—Delta Days and Game Days would have never happened without you, my expert assistant, producer, and friend. Thank you for always being willing to carry my bags even if it is off your jet!

Thank you to all my friends and family who dressed up, stood in the heat, swatted mosquitoes, and smiled pretty for the camera. I would be nowhere without your love and support.

Oxford Floral, Katie and David Naron, and Ashley—Thank you for always inspiring me but mostly just putting up with me. I am as always deeply grateful for you all.

Greg Bills—Your truck was the perfect tailgate. Thank you for sharing.

Babo—Thank you for being such a wonderful mother-in-law. I couldn't be any more fortunate to have you.

INDEX

NOTE: Page references in *italics* indicate photographs.

COME BACK SOON!